BRIDGING

THE CURRICULUM THROUGH ART

INTERDISCIPLINARY CONNECTIONS

PAMELA STEPHENS

NANCY WALKUP

CrystalProductions

Glenview, Illinois   Aspen, Colorado

Acknowledgements

North Texas Institute for Educators on
the Visual Arts

Transforming Education
through the Arts Challenge

Amon Carter Museum

Modern Art Museum of Fort Worth

Daggett Middle School
Fort Worth, Texas

Greenbriar Elementary School
Fort Worth, Texas

Mitchell Elementary School
Plano, Texas

North Hi Mount Elementary School
Fort Worth, Texas

Oakhurst Elementary School
Fort Worth, Texas

Shady Brook Elementary School
Bedford, Texas

ISBN 1-56290-270-9
Printed in Hong Kong

Contents

Presenting *Bridging the Curriculum Through Art: Lessons in Interdisciplinary Connections*

What is *Bridging the Curriculum through Art?*

The concept upon which *Bridging the Curriculum through Art* is based has come to be known by a variety of acronyms or terms such as Comprehensive Art Education (CAE), Discipline-Based Art Education (DBAE), or integrated curriculum. Fundamentally the same, each of these educational approaches maintains art as central to the curriculum, a bridge that unites content areas in logical and meaningful ways.

To understand these expansive concepts, it is essential to understand integration within the four foundational disciplines of art: art production, art history, art criticism, and aesthetics. These four disciplines encourage students to create, investigate, appreciate, and question art in ways that require critical thinking skills.

Through art production, students learn skills necessary to create art. Through art history, students gain knowledge about the contributions of art, artists, and cultures throughout time. Through art criticism, students learn to respond to art by describing, analyzing, interpreting, and making qualified judgments. Through aesthetics, students investigate the "big" questions about the nature of art and learn that the questioning process is as important as finding definitive answers.

DBAE, CAE, or integrated curriculum provides a model for extending interdisciplinary connections across the curriculum through art. With art as the central focus, the interconnected concepts of the curriculum become accessible and clear to students. Learning becomes cumulative and holistic when art is taught as a subject within the general curriculum. This interrelated curriculum strategy exemplifies substantive, measurable learning experiences.

Beyond creating an educational environment that contributes to improved learning outcomes, art-based learning also addresses the National Content Standards for Visual Arts, national educational guidelines that specify what students should know and be able to do in art. The National Content Standards for the Visual Arts correlate directly with the four disciplines of art.

Art Production

▶ Corresponding to the art discipline of production, the National Content Standards for the Visual Arts indicate that students "understand and apply art media, techniques, and processes."

Art History

▶ Coinciding with the discipline of art history, the National Content Standards require that students acquire an understanding of "the visual arts in relation to history and culture."

Art Criticism

▸ Equivalent to the discipline of art criticism, the National Content Standards direct that students "understand the structure and function of art" and that they "know a range of art subject matter, art symbols, and potential ideas."

Aesthetics

▸ Parallel to the art discipline of aesthetics, the National Content Standards necessitate that students "recognize the characteristics and merits of the artwork of others and themselves."

The National Content Standards for other subjects, such as language arts, mathematics, performing arts, science, and social studies also correlate with art, substantiating art's importance to the general curriculum. For example, placing events in sequential order, cause and effect relationships, and vocabulary acquisition are each invoked by art production. Art history teaches content objectives by utilizing sequencing and chronological order. Art criticism informs the objectives of main idea, point of view, description, analysis, and inference. The objectives of perceiving relationships and analyzing outcomes are key to the art discipline of aesthetics. Any variety of other reciprocal learning objectives is easily bridged with art across the curriculum.

What is included in *Bridging the Curriculum through Art?*

Bridging the Curriculum through Art focuses upon the critical relationship that comprehensive, quality art education has with curriculum content and learning outcomes. Included in this book are cross-curricular lessons developed and field-tested by art specialists and classroom teachers in a variety of educational settings. The lessons, each designed to deeply explore artists and works of art, are intended as a starting point for art exploration and can be easily implemented in long-range units of art-based study.

Bridging the Curriculum through Art includes:

▸ A brief historical background of National Content Standards and how these standards guide curriculum today

▸ Summarized lists of the National Content Standards for the Visual Arts, Language Arts, Mathematics, the Performing Arts, Science, and Social Studies

▸ Individual Chapters devoted to art-based lessons in language arts, mathematics, the performing arts, science, and social studies

▸ Step-by-step instructions for each art-based activity

▸ Reproducible worksheets for students

▸ Hints for promoting art programs

▸ A model and checklist for writing an art-based unit of study

How is *Bridging the Curriculum through Art* Used?

Bridging the Curriculum through Art is designed to assist teachers with development of art-centered lessons that contribute to integrated units of study. Divided into chapters, each chapter of the book concentrates on teaching one content area through meaningful exploration of the visual arts. Each chapter includes an overview, detailed and sequential instructions for activities, and in some instances, pages designed to be duplicated for classroom use as student worksheets.

While it should be noted that individual activities in this book may be used for stand alone lessons by any teacher, art specialists and classroom teachers are encouraged to use the activities as a basis for collaboratively planning and implementing in-depth units of art-centered study. During the planning process, teachers are advised to refer to the National Content Standards that are summarized in *Bridging the Curriculum through Art*. Reference to the National Content Standards better enables alignment among art and other curricula, thus promoting stronger connections and more opportunities for integrated learning. Art-based curriculum writing guidelines are also included in *Bridging the Curriculum through Art*. These guidelines may be used as a model for development of comprehensive, integrated lessons. A checklist for the guidelines is included as a quick reference tool. After using the guidelines to write units of study, the checklist will help determine any areas needing more emphasis.

To effectively use the art-based lessons in *Bridging the Curriculum through Art*, art reproductions are required. It is recommended that an assortment of art prints be used. Art postcards, slides, and color transparencies are other options.

Chapter 1
Summary: The National Content Standards

" The educational foundations of our society are presently being eroded by a rising tide of mediocrity that threatens our very future as a nation and a people . . . . We have, in effect, been committing an act of unthinking, unilateral educational disarmament. "

— *A Nation at Risk*
National Commission on Excellence in Education

Background

In 1983, with these sobering words from the National Commission on Excellence in Education and surrounded by growing concerns about the lack of quality educational preparation of America's young people, the United States began to rethink its educational systems and to face the challenges of the future. Fundamental to these challenges was identification of underlying factors contributing to success or lack of success of schools and students: readiness to learn, the dropout rate, student achievement and citizenship, teacher education and professional development, global academic ranking, safe schools, and community partnerships.

Some six years after the publication of *A Nation at Risk*, President George Bush called an education summit in 1989 to examine the issues and problems associated with achievement of academic excellence in public schools. The publication that came about from this summit, *The National Education Goals Report: Building a Nation of Learners*, provided a foundation of six expansive goals for what is now recognized as national content standards. Goals three and four of this document specifically spoke to academic competency and social achievements that were to be reached before the year 2000.

In 1990, *The National Education Goals* were outlined in Bush's State of the Union speech and congress created the National Education Goals Panel followed by the establishment of the National Council on Education Standards and Testing. Together they were directed to look at American education and to determine what should be taught, what students should know, and how they should be assessed. From the efforts of these two groups, national teacher organizations from a variety of content areas began to seek standards for their own fields. The *Curriculum and Evaluation Standards for School Mathematics*, published by the

National Council of Teachers of Mathematics in 1989 (prior to mandated standards), provided a model for those education groups that soon followed.

Content standards for each subject area are explicit and explain what students at each grade level should know and be able to do. The standards for each content area furnish a framework from which rigorous studies can be developed and implemented. They should not be confused, however, with scope and sequence or prescribed curriculum; rather, they are sets of goals designed as guidelines to direct the development of appropriate curricula.

The visual arts have benefited significantly from the development of national content standards. By specifying that students should learn not only to manipulate art materials, but that they should develop analytical and interpretive skills, explore historical and cultural relationships, acquire questioning abilities, and make meaningful connections with other disciplines, the national content standards invite the visual arts to be as academically challenging as other content areas.

The following lists of national content standards for the visual arts, language arts, mathematics, performing arts, science, and social studies are summarized for ready access and cross reference. Teachers are encouraged to seek the complete documents for more specific explanations of each standard.

Summary:
National Content Standards for the Visual Arts

These standards are drawn from *The National Standards for Arts Education*, 1994, which was written by the Consortium of National Arts Education Associations. The first five standards direct that students will experience and understand art in a variety of ways that encompass observing art, thinking and talking about art, and creating art. Standard 6 emphasizes connections to other content areas.

Students will:

Standard 1:	Understand and apply art media, techniques, and processes. (Making art)
Standard 2:	Understand the structure of art (elements of art and principles of design) and functions of art. (Art criticism)
Standard 3:	Know a range of art subject matter, art symbols, and potential ideas. (Art criticism)
Standard 4:	Understand the visual arts in relation to history and culture. (Art history)

Courtesy Dallas Museum of Art. Photo by Nancy Walkup.

Standard 5:	Recognize the characteristics and merits of the artwork of others and themselves. (Aesthetics)
Standard 6:	Understand connections among the various art forms and other disciplines.

Summary:
National Content Standards for Language Arts

The International Reading Association and the National Council of Teachers of English provide eight content standards in their document, *Standards for the English Language Arts*, 1996. These standards outline necessary competencies in reading, writing, and listening.

Students will:

Standard 1:	Show competence in the general skills and strategies of writing.
Standard 2:	Demonstrate proficiency in rhetoric and composition.
Standard 3:	Use correct grammar and mechanics in writing.
Standard 4:	Gather and use information for research.
Standard 5:	Show competence in the general skills and strategies of reading.
Standard 6:	Exhibit competence in the general skills and strategies for reading a variety of literary texts.
Standard 7:	Exhibit competence in the general skills and strategies for reading a variety of informational texts.
Standard 8:	Demonstrate competence in speaking and listening skills.

Summary:
National Content Standards for Mathematics

This summary is based chiefly upon the *Mathematics Framework for the 1996 National Assessment of Educational Progress* (NAEP). While Standards one through eight reflect most current thinking on what students should know and be able to do in mathematics, Standard nine addresses a broader awareness about mathematics and the content's connections to other disciplines.

Students will:

Standard 1: Understand and apply basic and advanced strategies to solve problems.

Standard 2: Understand and apply basic and advanced concepts of number properties.

Standard 3: Understand and apply basic and advanced procedures to perform computation.

Standard 4: Understand and apply basic and advanced concepts of measurement.

Standard 5: Understand and apply basic and advanced properties of geometry.

Standard 6: Understand and apply basic and advanced concepts of statistics and data analysis.

Standard 7: Understand and apply basic and advanced concepts of probability.

Standard 8: Understand and apply basic and advanced properties and functions of algebra.

Standard 9: Understand the nature and uses of mathematics.

Photo by Nancy Walkup.

Summary:
National Content Standards for Performing Arts

The content standards for the performing arts, like the visual arts content standards, are delineated in *The National Standards for Arts Education*, 1994. Written by the Consortium of National Arts Education Associations, the standards for dance, music, and theater are similar in their reach to the visual arts standards. Content standards for each of the performing arts contains reference to specific skills that relate to competence in that subject. Additionally, each set of standards has one broader criterion that indicates making connections to other content areas.

Dance

Students will:

Standard 1: Identify and demonstrate movement elements and skills in dance performance.

Standard 2: Understand choreographic principles, processes, and structures.

Standard 3: Explore dance as a way to create and communicate meaning.

Standard 4: Use critical and creative thinking skills.

Standard 5: Understand dance in relation to various cultures and historical periods.

Standard 6: Make connections between dance and healthful living.

Standard 7: Understand connections among the various art forms and other disciplines.

Music

Students will:

Standard 1: Sing alone and with others and use a varied repertoire.

Standard 2: Perform on instruments alone and with others and use a varied repertoire.

Standard 3: Improvise melodies, variations, and accompaniments.

Standard 4: Use specified guidelines to compose and arrange music.

Standard 5: Read and notate music.

Standard 6: Understand and apply suitable criteria to music and music performances.

Standard 7: Understand relationships between music, history, and culture.

Standard 8: Understand connections among the various art forms and other disciplines.

Theatre

Students will:

Standard 1: Show competence in scriptwriting.

Standard 2: Use acting skills.

Standard 3: Design and produce informal and formal productions.

Standard 4: Direct scenes and productions.

Standard 5: Understand how informal and formal theatre, film, television, and electronic media productions create and communicate meaning.

Standard 6: Know the context in which theatre, film, television, and electronic media are performed today and in the past.

Standard 7: Understand connections among the various art forms and other disciplines.

Summary:
National Content Standards for Social Studies

These National Content Standards for Social Studies were derived from *Expectations for Excellence: Curriculum Standards for Social Studies* written by the National Council of Social Studies. The Social Studies Content Standards identify thematic strands and specify what each student should know in each grade level in regard to each strand. Although strands are repeated in a variety of grade levels, content for the individual strands is grade-level appropriate and becomes more complex in upper grades.

Students will:

Standard 1: Explore the similarities and differences among cultures.

Standard 2: Use processes to interpret time, continuity, and change.

Standard 3: Understand that people, places, and environments reflect cultural values.

Standard 4: Know that people, place, and time influence individual development and identity.

Standard 5: Analyze how individuals, groups, and institutions impact culture.

Standard 6: Understand the roles that production, distribution, and consumption play in economic systems.

Standard 7: Analyze how power, authority, and governance meet the needs and wants of citizens.

Standard 8: Identify and interpret civic ideas and practices.

Summary:
National Content Standards for Science

The *National Education Science Standards* written by the National Research Council (1994) is the document from which these summarized content standards have been drawn. The National Content Standards for Science describe what students should know, understand, and be able to do in the field of science.

Students will understand:

Standard 1: Basic features of the Earth.

Standard 2: Fundamental Earth processes.

Standard 3: Composition and structure of the universe and the Earth's place in it.

Standard 4: Diversity and unity that characterize life.

Standard 5: Genetic transfer of biological characteristics.

Standard 6: The general structure and functions of cells.

Standard 7: That species depend on one another and on the environment for survival.

Standard 8: The cycling of matter and flow of energy through the living environment.

Standard 9: The basic concepts of evolution.

Standard 10: Basic concepts about the structure and properties of matter.

Standard 11: Energy types, sources, and conversions, and their relationship to heat and temperature.

Standard 12: Motion and the principles that explain it.

Standard 13: The kinds of forces that exist between objects and within atoms.

Standard 14: The nature of scientific knowledge.

Standard 15: The nature of scientific inquiry.

Standard 16: The scientific enterprise.

Chapter 2
Developing Art-Based,
Interdisciplinary Units of Study

"*Disciplinary integration in art is educationally desirable not only because it represents the actual ways in which artists and arts-related professionals experience art, but because it is an effective way to underscore and reinforce what is important.*"

— Stephen Mark Dobbs, 1998

Writing curricula need not be a burdensome task; rather, it should be considered as a learning experience for both students and their teachers. When students and teachers question and learn together, the value of learning is underscored and lifelong learning is modeled. Writing art-based units of study can be the catalyst for connected and profound learning. What would you like to know about an artist, an artwork, or an art style? Chances are students are curious about the same topics. Exploring questions of personal interest sparks the desire to learn more.

This chapter provides a suggested guideline for teachers who wish to develop art-based, interdisciplinary (or integrated) curricula. The foundations of curriculum writing, vocabulary of curriculum writing, a sequential outline, reproducible planning pages, and quick-reference checklists are provided. Teachers are encouraged to adapt these guidelines in ways that are most appropriate to individual teaching situations. Bear in mind that the activities offered in *Bridging the Curriculum through Art* should be considered as individual lessons. As such, these activities or lessons contribute to units of study; however, individual activities should not be considered complete within themselves.

Foundations

Art-based, integrated units of study are far-reaching, comprehensive, inclusive, and intellectually challenging. As with any other unit of study, art-based units are comprised of individual lessons linked together by a common theme related to the meaningful exploration of a subject. Art-based lessons go beyond the idea of "art projects" and encompass observing art, thinking about art, talking about art, writing about art, and creating art while making significant connections to other content areas.

The foundation of art-based, interdisciplinary curriculum should therefore provide opportunities for students to:

- Make art (art production).

- Interpret and judge artworks, both their own and the work of others (art criticism).

- Examine the historical, social, and cultural context of works of art (art history).

- Explore the nature and value of works of art (aesthetics).

- Make connections among the four foundational art disciplines as well as other content areas (interdisciplinary connections or integration).

- Demonstrate learning and complex understandings and skills.

Essential Vocabulary of Art-Based Curricula

Understanding the vocabulary of curriculum writing and the relationships between parts of a unit is critical to success. Additionally, all members of a collaborative curriculum-writing team should also have similar understandings of associated terminology. It is advisable that all team members review the vocabulary and come to a shared agreement about each term.

Listed here are essential vocabulary, brief definitions, and examples:

Alignment   Think of alignment in lesson writing as the matching of individual parts of the lesson so that all the parts create a unified whole. For example, assessment for a lesson should align with (or match) the learning objectives of the lesson. Objectives should align with national (and state or local) content standards.

In relation to a unit of study, alignment suggests that the various parts of the unit should align (be continuous and orderly while meeting content standards) so that the lessons flow smoothly and naturally.

Assessment   Various ways to check for learning. Assessment should always align with objectives; therefore, objectives should be measurable. Assessment measures the degree to which an objective has been met. Additionally, assessment should include opportunities for student self-assessment and reflection upon personal learning.

Lesson   A lesson is an individual section of a unit of study. Lessons are not necessarily time-sensitive and can cover more than one class session. Lessons contribute to the deeper exploration of a theme or connecting idea within a unit. In integrated learning environments, lessons meaningfully link together (align) in a way that solidifies interdisciplinary connections among content areas. At least one lesson relating to each of the four foundational disciplines of art (aesthetics, art criticism, art history, and production) should be included in a well-rounded unit of art-based study.

Objective   An objective is measurable and clearly states what it is that students will learn. Here is an example of a measurable objective:

Students will respond to philosophical questioning with compelling reasons in regard to the strengths and weaknesses of an artist's work. (Note that "compelling" provides the objective with a suggested range of measurement.)

Theme   Themes, as opposed to topics, are broad concepts or connecting ideas that typically are stated as a phrase or sentence and frequently include an action verb. Themes are also called enduring ideas, key concepts, overarching concepts, or umbrella ideas to name but a few synonyms.

A good example of a theme was an exhibition at the Fort Worth Museum of Science and History, *Finding Your Way*. This theme was used to explore the senses and how people utilize those senses to navigate through life.

Topic

Topics, as opposed to themes, are narrowly defined subjects. Whereas themes can expand to cover a wide variety of content areas, usually a topic will not lend itself to deep exploration across the curriculum.

An example of a topic is: pumpkins. It would be very difficult to develop significant and meaningful connections to art and other content areas with the limited idea of pumpkins.

Unit of study

A unit of study is sometimes simply called curriculum. Units of study are comprised of individual lessons. At least one lesson relating to each of the four foundational disciplines of art (aesthetics, art criticism, art history, and production) should be included in a well-rounded unit of art-based of study.

Courtesy Amon Carter Museum, Fort Worth, Texas. Photo by Nancy Walkup.

The Parts of an Art-Based Interdisciplinary Unit of Study

Designing an art-based, integrated unit of study requires thoughtful planning and collaboration among art teachers and teachers from other content areas. As you begin to undertake writing such a curriculum, think about the critical components of the unit and ask some questions in relation to the discriminate parts. The questions provided here should direct your initial development of the unit of study.

Component	Question
Identification of a theme	What is the overarching idea that will tie integrated learning together?
Identification of artworks	What works of art can be meaningfully explored that will address questions related to the theme?
Identification of objectives (one for each lesson)	What measurable learning is it that students should demonstrate in art and other content areas? What is it that you really want students to learn or know about?
Development of lessons	What activities can be related to a unit designed to help students find meaning in art and other content areas? How will the integrated lessons support the meaningful exploration of the theme? What resources will be required? What motivation will prompt investigation? Are each of the four disciplines of art represented with at least one meaningful activity within the unit?
Alignment of objectives and assessment within each lesson	How will student learning be measured to reflect accurately the stated objectives?
Alignment of content standards between and among subject areas	How will content standards for visual arts and other content standards be matched and met?

Guidelines for Writing an Art-Based Unit of Study
Step I: Identify a Theme and Artworks

A unit may begin through one of two approaches. The first method is to begin with a theme. Themes are sometimes referred to as enduring ideas, key concepts, overarching concepts, or umbrella ideas. After a theme is ascertained, the next step is to select artworks that best address the theme. Remember that you do not necessarily need to like a work for it to be beneficial to art exploration. Avoid identifying works of art that superficially illustrate an idea; instead, seek artwork that will stimulate inquiry and offer thought-provoking investigation of the theme.

For example, if the theme *Playing the Game* is determined, then works of art should focus upon what is meant by "playing" or "games." What is "playing?" What is a "game?" Is playing always for fun? When is a game not a game? How have artists presented playing and games throughout time? What do games tell us about time? Place? Culture?

The second approach is just opposite of the first. With the second approach, works of art are chosen and then a connecting theme is determined. Again, avoid using works of art to illustrate an idea. For example, if a variety of images of buildings are available, how are those buildings alike? Different? What do they express about the society or culture that constructed them? What do they tell about the time in which they were built? From this exploration, perhaps the theme of *Building for the Future* would become the basis of the unit of study.

No matter which of these two approaches for developing the unit of study is chosen, the underlying motivation for instruction is to teach through the artworks, to examine and find meaning, and to connect to other content areas.

Step II: Identification of Objectives

One clear learning objective should be stated for each lesson within a unit of study. Learning objectives should be invoked by these two questions:

▶ What is it that you really want students to know?

▶ How will you know that students have learned what you intended?

In addition, learning objectives should directly relate to what students will be expected to learn and how they will demonstrate that understanding. For these reasons, it is very important that learning objectives be distinct and measurable. Each lesson within a unit of study

should have its own distinct and measurable objective.

Distinct means that the learning objective clearly states one idea that will be taught. Measurable means that the objective indicates how students will demonstrate competency. Here is an example of a distinct and measurable learning objective:

▶ Students will communicate persuasive interpretations about the artwork based upon the political ideas of the time.

This objective is distinct because it isolates what the students will be charged with learning through art criticism and history or social studies (interpreting artwork based upon the political ideas of the time). The objective is measurable because it states how the students will be assessed (communicating persuasively). The adjective "persuasive" is necessary; otherwise, assessment would hinge solely upon students making interpretations without regard to how thoroughly an interpretation is supported by facts.

A word of caution: often activities are inadvertently labeled as learning objectives. Here are two examples of activities masquerading as learning objectives:

▶ Students will create a diorama about art and ecology.

▶ Students will write a critical review.

If the activity within a lesson is to create a diorama or write a review, the learning objectives would be better stated like this:

▶ Students will competently demonstrate an understanding of how artists identify and address ecological issues.

▶ Students will effectively describe and analyze a masterwork.

These are distinct and measurable objectives that lead to the activities of diorama and critical review.

In writing a unit of study, each lesson should have its own objective. Each objective should link (align) to each of the other objectives within the unit. All objectives should support the common theme and meaningful exploration of art.

Step III: Alignment of Objectives and Assessment

After determining measurable objectives, assessment should not be a difficult duty to fulfill. The learning objective should imply a range of what the assessment will be. Consider again this distinct and measurable learning objective:

> Students will competently demonstrate an understanding of how artists identify and address ecological issues.

"Competently" becomes the pivotal term in this learning objective. Competence does *not* suggest mastery. Competence suggests degrees of understanding. What then is demonstrated competence? One way to approach this is through the development of a rubric. (A complete definition of rubric and a sample rubric for a unit of study are included in the Vocabulary section of *Bridging Curriculum through Art*).

Rubrics provide a range of measurement for demonstration of student competence. Such a range might be (1) below expectations, (2) meets expectations, or (3) exceeds expectations. Competence then could be measured as:

> **Below Expectations**: not providing supporting evidence of knowledge about the ways that artists identify and address ecological issues.

> **Meets Expectations**: provides some supporting evidence of knowledge about the ways that artists identify and address ecological issues.

> **Exceeds Expectations**: provides a variety of supporting evidence of knowledge about the ways that artists identify and address ecological issues.

Using this rubric as an assessment key allows for greater flexibility in measuring demonstrated competency. With this sort of assessment, every student can be scored as an individual learner with varied responses rather than having only one acceptable answer that all students must produce. Moreover, students can also use the rubric for self-assessment and reflection upon learning.

Step IV: Development of Lessons

Now that a theme has been determined, artworks have been selected, and learning objectives and assessment have been considered, the next step is to design or choose an activity that best teaches the stated objective. If selecting an activity from *Bridging the Curriculum through Art*, take into account how that activity will meet the stated objective. If designing an original activity, keep in mind that art activities should address one of the four foundational art disciplines (art history, art criticism, aesthetics, or production) while connecting in meaningful ways to other content areas. Sometimes the connections can be as subtle as playing an art game that requires philosophical contemplation; other times the connections can be as overt as requiring students to locate places or time periods in social studies textbooks.

After the activity is selected or designed, details for preparation and presentation must be decided. These details include identifying and securing materials, tools, and resources as well as ascertaining vocabulary that will be new for students. These questions should prompt organization of details.

> What materials and tools will be required to teach the lesson? Are the materials and tools readily available? If not, how and when will they be obtained?

> How will the materials and tools be prepared? Who will prepare the materials and tools required to teach the lesson? When and where will the materials and tools be prepared?

> What resources will be needed to teach the lesson? Resources include such materials as study prints, posters, books, slides, videos, color transparencies, postcards, or Internet.

> How will the resources be used for best advantage to stimulate student interest in the lesson?

> What new vocabulary related to each lesson will students be required to know? How will new vocabulary be conveyed to students?

Step V: Alignment of Content Standards

The National Content Standards for each subject area are valuable tools in the development of lessons and art-based, interdisciplinary units of study. As documents that indicate what students should know and do in each subject, the standards provide a framework from which interdisciplinary lessons and units of study emerge.

It is highly recommended that teachers become familiar with the content standards for all subject areas or refer to the content standards often. A summary of many of the content standards is listed for easy reference in the previous chapter. Complete and detailed lists of all content standards are available from a variety of sources.

The bottom line for checking that individual art lessons within a unit of study meet the requirement of alignment with the National Content Standards for Visual Arts is simply to identify the content standard or standards and ask how that standard has been fulfilled. A similar process should be utilized for other subject areas as well.

Unit Planning Worksheet

Theme of Unit

Lesson 1	_____
	_____
Objective	_____
	_____
Artwork(s)	_____
	_____
Resources	_____
	_____
Activity	_____
	_____
Materials	_____
	_____
Assessment	_____
	_____

Lesson 2	_____
	_____
Objective	_____
	_____
Artwork(s)	_____
	_____
Resources	_____
	_____
Activity	_____
	_____
Materials	_____
	_____
Assessment	_____
	_____

Lesson 3	_____
	_____
Objective	_____
	_____
Artwork(s)	_____
	_____
Resources	_____
	_____
Activity	_____
	_____
Materials	_____
	_____
Assessment	_____
	_____

Lesson 4	_____
	_____
Objective	_____
	_____
Artwork(s)	_____
	_____
Resources	_____
	_____
Activity	_____
	_____
Materials	_____
	_____
Assessment	_____
	_____

Lesson Planning Worksheet

Lesson Title
Theme of Unit

Objective _____

Students will _____

_____

Materials & _____

Preparation _____

_____

_____

Resources _____

_____

_____

_____

Motivation _____

_____

_____

_____

Vocabulary _____

_____

_____

_____

Artwork(s) _____

_____

_____

Activity _____

_____

_____

_____

_____

_____

_____

_____

_____

Assessment _____

_____

_____

_____

National Content Standards _____

_____

_____

_____

Checklist for an Art-Based Interdisciplinary Unit of Study

This checklist is a quick reference for determining if all necessary parts of a unit of study have been included.

	Yes	No
A unifying theme that will tie all lessons together has been stated	☐	☐
A distinct and measurable objective is stated for each lesson	☐	☐
Artworks have been chosen for each lesson	☐	☐
Resources have been identified for each lesson	☐	☐
Materials have been identified for each lesson	☐	☐
Assessment for each lesson aligns with the objective for the lesson	☐	☐
Each lesson meaningfully links to the others while supporting exploration of artworks and the stated theme	☐	☐
Art production is provided in one lesson	☐	☐
Art criticism is provided in one lesson	☐	☐
Aesthetics is provided in one lesson	☐	☐
Art history is provided in one lesson	☐	☐
Meaningful connections to other content areas are maintained	☐	☐
Content within each lesson is aligned with the National Content Standards	☐	☐
Lessons flow naturally and meaningfully together while supporting the theme	☐	☐

Checklist for a Complete Art Lesson

This checklist is a quick reference for determining if all necessary parts of an art lesson have been included.

	Yes	No
A theme that will tie all the lessons together has been stated	☐	☐
A distinct and measurable objective is clearly stated	☐	☐
Artwork that will be explored is identified	☐	☐
A significant art activity is selected or designed and includes one of the four foundational disciplines of art	☐	☐
Materials and tools have been identified	☐	☐
Preparation of materials and tools has been considered	☐	☐
Resources have been identified	☐	☐
Uses of resources for motivation of students have been considered	☐	☐
New vocabulary has been identified	☐	☐
Assessment aligns with the stated objective	☐	☐
Content of the lesson aligns with the National Content Standards for Visual Arts and other subjects	☐	☐

Chapter 3
Art and Language Arts

" There is only one incontrovertible conclusion to be reached. The arts are not a frill; they are an essential part of language."

— Ernest Boyer, 1987

Art and Language Arts

Both the visual arts and language arts are chiefly concerned with communication via seeing, hearing, and speaking. While visual arts, as the title implies, tend to address those concepts explored through visual observation, other communication skills are utilized as well. These other communication methods include reading, writing, listening, and speaking. Much the same as the skills taught through language arts concepts, the visual arts encourage students to observe, analyze, interpret, and make reasoned judgments about art and artists. Reading or writing about an art object or artist, listening to what others have to say about art and artists, or making reasoned judgments supports quality art learning, but, just as importantly provides quality language arts connections as well.

Competence in Writing

Writing skills include strategies involved with planning (i.e., prewriting); drafting and revising; writing in a variety of formats such as narrative, descriptive, persuasive, and classificatory; editing and publishing; and evaluating. Using writing strategies to explore works of art provides a framework that allows deeper exploration of art and artists while reinforcing language art skills.

Rhetoric and Composition

Writing about artists and works of art furnishes students with opportunities to develop and use descriptive language that clarifies and enriches communication. Moreover, writing about art and artists provides students with occasions to visually identify topics, main ideas, and related ideas then to express those concepts in written forms (topic sentences, main ideas of paragraphs, and related ideas between paragraphs). Exploring artworks in depth and searching for clues within the art object helps students to use supporting evidence to justify statements. What better way to learn about

Art and Language Arts

Photo by Nancy Walkup.

sequencing than to write about the processes artists use to create art? Other language arts concepts readily correlated with investigation of art include use of analogies, paraphrasing, and anecdotes; recognition of the differences between phrases and sentences; restatement of ideas; and development of personal style to convey ideas.

Correct Grammar and Mechanics of the Written Word

When writing about art and artists, students use the same grammar and mechanics of writing that are used in language arts classes. Providing opportunities for students to delve into artworks and biographies of artists bolsters understanding of art while underscoring the importance of using correct grammar and writing structures for better communication of ideas. As in language arts, writing in the visual arts classroom entails the correct use of parts of speech, proper capitalization, and accurate punctuation.

Research

Gathering information about artists and their work requires that students utilize a variety of strategies for research. These strategies include identification of topics for investigation (e.g., brainstorming, listing questions, or using idea webs); gathering information from diverse sources such as dictionaries, encyclopedias, books, or the Internet; using multiple kinds of information ranging from written material to maps, photos, and charts to supplement a research topic; creating notes, charts, graphs, or other information to compile research information; and bringing together all pertinent information to write about a topic.

Reading from a Variety of Texts

Works of art are as diverse as the artists who create them. Learning to read an art object requires interpretative skills that can be extended from one style to another. Much like the differences between newspaper articles and literature or novels and poetry, fluency in reading artwork requires identifying, recognizing, and understanding the fundamental purposes of each. For example, reading a classical sculpture requires a similar approach to reading a pop art painting; however, the characteristics that make the sculpture "classical" or that make the painting "pop art" are quite different. Learning to read an art object helps students draw conclusions and make inferences, differentiate between fact and opinion, and show different points of view based upon explicit and implicit information found within works of art.

Speaking and Listening

Talking about art and artists provides students freedom to contribute to group discussions, formulate and ask appropriate questions in class, and respond to questions and comments while giving reasons in support of opinions. Additionally, talking about art and listening to others sharpens skills so that students learn not to interrupt others, to ask well-thought-out questions at the correct time, to confirm understanding, and to give feedback to the speaker. Art discussions, especially those involving criticism or aesthetics, can be especially rich and help students identify specific ways language can be used to effectively communicate agreement or disagreement with ideas.

Photo by Nancy Walkup

Prose and Poetry

Prose — typically characterized as ordinary or daily language, the language of newspapers, magazines, short stories, novels, and conversation — conveys or suggests a straightforward approach to communicating about a topic. In the visual arts, prose is the language of newspaper or magazine critics who inform their readership about exhibitions or other topics in the fine arts. Prose is usually the communication of aestheticians who challenge us to think about the big picture or answer questions about "what is art?" Prose provides a means for students to contrast and compare works of art, persuade others about their own ideas, describe artworks, and narrate stories found in art objects.

Poetry — characterized by condensed use of vivid language — is frequently more intense or colorful than prose. Because of this divergent use of language, poetic verse offers students opportunities to explore works of art and communicate about them in many different ways that extend beyond the confines of descriptive, persuasive, classificatory, or narrative writing. Using poetry formats when writing about art objects invites deep reflection that can result in intense expression.

Both prose and poetry provide diverse but practical formats that are readily applicable to the interpretation of works of art. Both traditional and nontraditional prose and poetry formats can be adapted for art interpretation. Prose formats include interview outlines, letters, Venn diagrams, and deciphering fact from opinion. Poetry formats include acrostic, cinquain, haiku, upside-down

triangle, and W poems. These are but a few language arts frameworks that can be used to stimulate careful art observation, contemplative interpretation, and creative writing. These prose and poetry formats, along with instructions for their individual use, are included in this section.

Resources

The Oxford Treasury of Time Poems. (1998). Oxford University Press.

Stephens, P.G. and Green, S.D. (1997, November). Deciphering Fact and Opinion. *School Arts*, 40-41.

Interviewing an Artist

Letters: Formal and Informal

Venn Diagram

Classificatory Persuasive

Fact and Opinion

Acrostic Poems

Cinquain

Haiku

Upside-Down Triangle Poem

W Poem

Art teachers meet with sculptor Jesus Moroles to explore ways that students can interview artists. Photo by Nancy Walkup

Interviewing an Artist

Interviews provide factual information to the reader that relate to who, what, when, where, and why. When interviewing an artist, the same questions apply. As a reporter, these questions should be asked in relation to the artist's history and artwork.

The interview format can be easily applied to art research. Using who, what, when, where, and why as an outline, students working individually or in groups can prepare their own questions from each category and seek answers in books or on the Internet. After answering their questions with the available resources, articles can be written about artists and their artwork.

Directions

▶ Students can either work independently or in small groups.

▶ Assign the name of an artist or art professional to each student or group.

▶ Provide the artist interview worksheet and one or more images of the artist's work.

▶ Ask students to carefully explore the artwork and formulate questions for each category about the art.

▶ Next, ask students to formulate questions for each category that explore the artist's history.

▶ After all questions are formulated, provide background information about the artist and artwork.

▶ Ask students to use the background information to answer as many questions as possible. Any questions that are unanswered should be researched in books or on the Internet.

▶ Using the information gleaned from their own inquiry and responses, ask students to write a factual article such as might be found in a magazine or newspaper. Avoid the use of opinions. Head the sections of the article "About the Artist" and "About the Art."

▶ Display images of the art and artist alongside student-written articles.

Suggested works of art

▶ Any artwork that has information available about the art and artist

Interviewing an Artist

Look carefully at the work of art.

In the first column, write two or more questions for each category about the work of art.

In the second column, write two or more questions for each category about the artist.

Questions about the work of art	Questions about the artist
Category 1: Who?	Category 1: Who?
Category 2: What?	Category 2: What?
Category 3: When?	Category 3: When?
Category 4: Where?	Category 4: Where?
Category 5: Why?	Category 5: Why?
Category 6: Something else I would like to ask is…	Category 6: Something else I would like to ask is…

After locating the answers to your questions, use the information to write a newspaper or magazine article about the artwork and artist. Be careful to use only factual information in your written work.

Letters: Formal and Informal

Photo by Nancy Walkup

Letters: Formal and Informal

Letters convey our thoughts in a different style than interviews or articles. Letters can be businesslike (or formal) such as letters to the editor, letters requesting information, or letters that attempt to persuade. Letters can also be friendly in tone (informal) such as the kind written to family members or friends.

Letters follow guidelines that suggest their content, recipient, and sender. All letters should include a heading, date, salutation (greeting), body, closing, and signature. The difference between the types of letters is the language used. The closing of a formal business letter wherein the writer tries to persuade the recipient to change an opinion should be along the lines of "Sincerely" or "Sincerely yours." The closing of a business letter will be far different than the closing of a letter between friends or family members. A friendly letter will likely conclude with "Love" or some other term or phrase of endearment.

Formal letter

▸ Students should work individually.

▸ Provide each student with a reproduction of a work of art and a letter worksheet.

▸ Ask students to write a letter to the editor or director of a museum.

▸ The topic of the letter should be persuasive such as convincing the editor to publicize the artwork or asking the museum director to purchase the artwork for the museum.

▸ Display the completed letters next to the works of art each discuss.

Informal letter

▸ Students should work individually.

▸ Provide each student with a reproduction of a work of art and a letter worksheet.

▸ Ask students to select a character within the artwork from whose point-of-view the letter will be written.

▸ The informal letter can be written to a family member, an advice columnist, or a friend.

▸ Display the completed letters next to the works of art that have been explored.

Suggested works of art

▸ Works of art that include identifiable characters such as people or animals

▸ *Zebras and Hyenas*, Melissa Miller

▸ *Woman with Blueberries*, Patrick DesJarlait

▸ *Dance for the Hunt*, Lee N. Smith III

▸ *The Songs My Father Taught Me Are the Songs I Teach My Son*, Ricardo Ruiz

▸ *Four Seasons*, John Biggers

Write a Letter

Writer's name and address

_____

_____

_____

Date

_____

Recipient's name and address

_____

_____

_____

Salutation

_____ :

Body of letter

_____

_____

_____

_____

_____

_____

_____

_____

Closing

_____ ,

Signature of writer

_____

Venn Diagram

Interviewing an Artist

Letters: Formal and Informal

Venn Diagram

Classificatory Persuasive

Fact and Opinion

Acrostic Poems

Cinquain

Haiku

Upside-Down Triangle Poem

W Poem

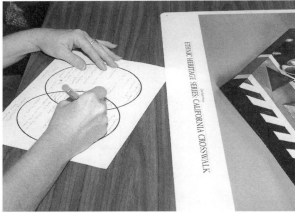

Photo by Nancy Walkup

Venn Diagram

John Venn (1834-1923) was an English priest, philosopher, and teacher who wrote several books on logic and created what has become widely known today as the Venn Diagram. Venn Diagrams are commonly used to describe or compare and contrast characteristics of events, objects, people, situations, wants, ideas, or concepts.

Venn's original diagrams include three intersecting circles. A simpler Venn, however, uses only two circles. When using Venn Diagrams to explore artists, works of art, art styles, or other art concepts, the two overlapping circles provide a visual way to list and sort individual characteristics. The intersecting portion of the circles provides a place to list similarities between the two.

Venn Diagrams are not meant to be an end product; rather, they should be considered a prewriting activity that leads to organization of thought. Implementation of Venn Diagrams helps students to identify unique characteristics about art topics, to describe those characteristics, and then to find similarities between diverse subjects. Additionally, Venn Diagrams help students to group information into logical order for cohesive writing.

Directions

- ▶ Place students in teams of two or in small collaborative groups.

- ▶ Ask one student to act as the recorder of information.

- ▶ Provide two art reproductions. Other art topics such as brief biographies of artists or articles about art styles also can be used.

- ▶ Provide a Venn Diagram worksheet for each team or group.

- ▶ In the left circle, ask the recorder to enter the title of the first work of art (or artist's name or art style).

- ▶ In the right circle, enter the title of the second work of art. (or artist's name or art style).

- ▶ Tell students to closely observe the first artwork and list all unique characteristics about the work in the first circle.

- ▶ Repeat this process for the second work of art.

- ▶ Ask students to determine what the works have in common and to write these commonalities in the area where the circles overlap.

- ▶ Use the recorded information as an outline to write a report that contains three or more paragraphs. Paragraph one should describe the first object based upon the unique characteristics of that object listed in the left circle. Paragraph two should describe the second work of art based upon the unique characteristics listed in the right circle. The final paragraph should discuss what the two diverse works of art have in common.

Alternate

Instead of the Venn Diagram worksheet, place two overlapping hula hoops on the floor.

Suggested Works of Art

- ▶ Any works that have both similarities and differences

Venn Diagram

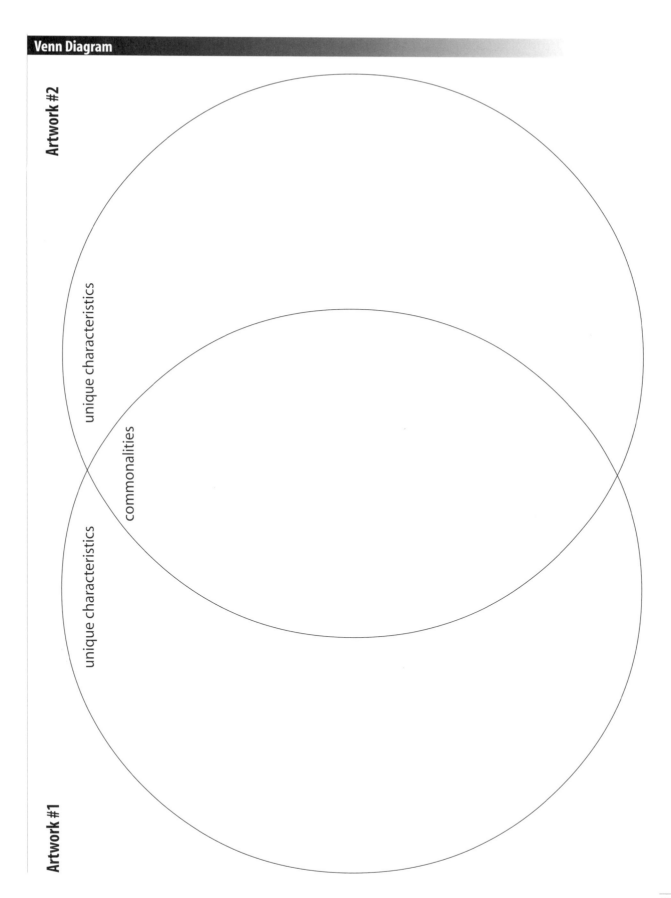

Artwork #2

unique characteristics

commonalities

unique characteristics

Artwork #1

Classificatory Persuasive

Photo by Nancy Walkup.

Classificatory Persuasive

Another use of the Venn Diagram is to assist with classificatory persuasive writing activities. Classificatory persuasive activities go beyond contrast and compare to require students to convince readers or listeners about a topic, idea, or opinion.

Directions

▶ Assign students to teams of two.

▶ Provide two art reproductions.

▶ Review the elements of art and principles of design.

▶ Distribute copies of the Venn Diagram.

▶ Ask students to record the title and unique characteristics of the first work of art inside the left circle and the title and unique characteristics of the second work of art inside the right circle.

▶ Use the overlapping section of the Venn Diagram to record similarities between the two works of art. Remind students to include the elements of art and principles of design in their lists.

▶ Distribute the classificatory persuasive worksheet.

▶ Tell students to use the Venn Diagram as a reference to write four paragraphs. The first paragraph should tell how the elements of art and principles of design are used in the first artwork. The second paragraph should tell how the elements of art and principles of design are used in the second artwork. The third paragraph should tell what the two artworks have in common. The last paragraph should attempt to persuade the audience that one of the artworks uses the elements of art and principles of design better.

▶ Ask teams to share their work aloud.

▶ Display the classificatory persuasive writings alongside the works of art they discuss.

Classificatory Persuasive

Write a paragraph of three or more sentences that tells how the elements of art and principles of design are used in the first work of art. Be sure to include the title of the artwork.

Write a paragraph of three or more sentences that tells how the elements of art and principles of design are used in the second work of art. Be sure to include the title of the artwork.

Write a paragraph of three or more sentences that tells what the two artworks have in common.

Write a paragraph of three or more sentences that persuades the reader or listeners that one artwork uses the elements of art and principles of design better.

Fact and Opinion

Photograph of Nancy Walkup with students taken at the Amon Carter Museum. Amon Carter Museum, Fort Worth, Texas.

Fact and Opinion

One language arts concept that often confuses students is differentiating between fact and opinion. Facts are defined as something that is true or can be proven to be true or real or in existence. Opinions tend to be classified as viewpoints or judgments that cannot be proven to be true. Works of art assist with visualization of the rules that govern these contradicting notions.

Directions

▶ Display an art reproduction so that it is visible to the entire class. Taping the reproduction to a chalkboard, dry erase board, or bulletin board works well.

▶ If using a chalk or dry erase board, write the word "Fact" to the right of the image and the word "Opinion" to the left. If using the bulletin board, create posters with the words and attach the posters to either side of the reproduction.

▶ Distribute 3 x 5-in. note cards to students.

▶ Ask each student to write one statement about the art image on a card.

▶ When ample time has been allowed for each student to compose a statement, ask students to individually read their statements aloud to the class and then classify the statement as either fact or opinion.

▶ Tape the statement on either the fact or opinion side of the art reproduction.

▶ Ask students to decide if the statement has been correctly classified. Require justified reasons for placement in either category.

▶ When most students agree and have given valid reasons for the placement of the statement, continue until all statements have been read, sorted, and justified.

▶ Distribute the fact and opinion worksheet.

▶ From this point, students should work individually.

▶ Ask students to review the facts and opinions posted with the art reproduction.

▶ Tell students to select five facts and five opinions from the lists and to record them on their worksheet.

▶ Using the five selected facts, write a factual paragraph about the work of art.

▶ Using the five selected opinions, write a paragraph based upon opinions.

▶ Display the writings near the art reproduction. How do both writings tell about the artwork? How are the writings different?

Fact and Opinion

Title of the work of art _____

Name of the artist _____

Write five facts about this work of art.

1. _____
2. _____
3. _____
4. _____
5. _____

Use the facts you have listed to write a paragraph about the work of art.

_____
_____
_____
_____
_____
_____

Write five opinions about this work of art.

1. _____
2. _____
3. _____
4. _____
5. _____

Use the opinions you have listed to write a paragraph about the work of art.

_____
_____
_____
_____
_____
_____

Acrostic Poems

Interviewing an Artist

Letters: Formal and Informal

Venn Diagram

Classificatory Persuasive

Fact and Opinion

Acrostic Poems

Cinquain

Haiku

Upside-Down Triangle Poem

W Poem

Acrostic Poems

An acrostic is a poem that is usually nonrhyming. The first letter of each line of an acrostic creates a word, phrase, or sentence that can be read vertically down the page. The horizontal lines of an acrostic can be phrases, parts of sentences, or complete sentences. The most interesting acrostic poems are usually created with sentences that begin on one line and end on another.

Here is an acrostic poem that was written by Lewis Carroll:

A poem that

C an be read across and

R ead downwards. The first

O r last, or another

S pecific letter will

T ell its own story

I n a word, a name, or a

C atch phrase.

Directions

▸ Assign students to collaborative groups of three or four.

▸ Provide an art image for each group to explore.

▸ Provide the acrostic worksheet and another sheet of paper for brainstorming.

▸ Ask one student in each group to be the recorder for that group. The recorder will write the words and phrases that the collaborative group generates.

▸ Ask the recorders to write the title of their work of art vertically on the acrostic worksheet. One letter should be written in each blank on the worksheet.

▸ Instruct students to observe the assigned artwork and consider the title. How does the title tell about the art object? What clues found in the work of art suggest or support the title?

▸ Using each letter of the title, instruct students to find a clue within the artwork and to brainstorm phrases that begin with that letter.

▸ After brainstorming, tell students to review their phrases.

▸ Select the best phrases for each letter of the title.

▸ Additional words or punctuation should be added to make the acrostic readable and interesting.

▸ How does the acrostic tell about the artwork and title?

Suggested Works of Art

▸ Works with brief titles

Acrostic Poem

Cinquain

Interviewing an Artist

Letters: Formal and Informal

Venn Diagram

Classificatory Persuasive

Fact and Opinion

Acrostic Poems

Cinquain

Haiku

Upside-Down Triangle Poem

W Poem

Cinquain

A cinquain is a five-line stanza that usually does not rhyme. The first line contains a single word — a noun; the second line contains two words — both adjectives; the third line is composed of three action verbs; the fourth line is a four-word phrase; and the fifth line is a single synonym for the original noun.

Here is an example of a cinquain:

Poem

Picturesque   Descriptive

Expressing   Reflecting   Nonrhyming

Paint a word picture

Cinquain

Directions

▶ Assign students to teams of two.

▶ Provide an assortment of art images from which each student may select one.

▶ Provide a cinquain worksheet for each student.

▶ Review the parts of speech used in the cinquain format:

Noun: a word that is the name of a person, place, or thing

Adjective: a word that describes or modifies a noun

Action verb (gerund): a word that expresses an act and ends with "-ing"

Phrase: words that do not form a complete sentence

Synonym: a word that means about the same as another word

▶ One student in each team will be the observer and the other will be the recorder.

▶ After the observer has had ample time to look at the art object, the recorder will prompt the observer for a response by reading aloud one line of the worksheet, waiting for a response, and writing it onto the worksheet. This process is repeated for each line until the cinquain is complete.

▶ When the first cinquain is complete, the observer and recorder change roles.

▶ After all teams have finished their cinquains, read the poems aloud.

▶ What information has been learned about the artwork that might otherwise have been overlooked?

Suggested Works of Art

▶ Representational works for younger students

▶ More challenging works, such as nonobjective or abstract, for older students

Cinquain

Title of the work of art _____

Name of the artist _____

Noun

Adjective   Adjective

Action verb   Action verb   Action verb

Four-word phrase

Synonym

Haiku

Interviewing an Artist

Letters: Formal and Informal

Venn Diagram

Classificatory Persuasive

Fact and Opinion

Acrostic Poems

Cinquain

Haiku

Upside-Down Triangle Poem

W Poem

Haiku

Haiku is one of the most important forms of traditional Japanese poetry. Haiku is a contemplative, unrhymed verse that attempts to link nature to human life. A well-written haiku creates tension by contrasting ideas such as inactivity and movement, change and stability, or nature and humanity. Haiku poems always maintain an economy of words.

General rules govern the writing of haiku poetry. These rules are:

- A poem should consist of three lines and contain seventeen syllables.
- The first line of a haiku poem contains five syllables and usually indicates "when."
- The second line contains seven syllables and usually indicates "where."
- The third line contains five syllables and usually indicates "what."
- There should be a cutting or division between the two contrasting parts of the poem. In English, the first or second line (but not both) can end with a colon or a dash to show this cutting.
- First-person accounts are avoided.
- A kigo (season word) is included but should not be obvious.

- Present tense is used.
- Metaphors and similes are avoided.

This is an example of a haiku written by Basho, a Japanese master of haiku.

An old pond,

A frog jumps in —

The sound of water.

Directions

- Students may work independently or in teams of two.
- Provide haiku worksheets.
- Review the guidelines for creating a haiku.
- Discuss the idea of "kigo" and brainstorm some seasonal symbols that might not be obvious. For example, snow would be an obvious kigo for winter whereas furry animals might be a less obvious symbol.
- Provide examples of the use of present tense such as "a frog jumps in."
- Practice creating five-syllable lines that suggest "when."
- Practice creating seven-syllable lines that suggest "where."
- Practice creating five-syllable lines that suggest "what."
- Distribute appropriate study prints or other reproductions.
- Instruct students to observe the artwork carefully and then to identify a kigo that is not obvious.
- Use the haiku worksheet to write the poem.
- How has the haiku helped you to explore a part of the artwork you might otherwise have overlooked? How has it helped you to discover meaning in the artwork?

Suggested Works of Art

- Any work that suggests a season or time

Haiku

Title of the work of art _____

Name of the artist _____

Season _____

Kigo _____

When _____

Where _____

What _____

Upside-Down Triangle Poem

Interviewing an Artist

Letters: Formal and Informal

Venn Diagram

Classificatory Persuasive

Fact and Opinion

Acrostic Poems

Cinquain

Haiku

Upside-Down Triangle Poem

W Poem

Upside-Down Triangle Poem

An upside-down triangle poem can be either rhyming or nonrhyming. This format is called an upside-down triangle because it is constructed in the shape of an inverted triangle. Each line of an upside-down triangle poem contains the same number of words as the line number. For example, line one (which is at the base of the poem) has only one word while line eight (which is at the top of the poem) contains eight words. Each line, therefore, becomes progressively longer by one word. Usually upside-down triangle poems can be read two ways: from top to bottom (longest line to shortest line) or bottom to top (shortest line to longest line)

This upside-down triangle poem is about cave paintings and was written by a fifth-grade student:

Hunting, food, clothing, and blankets from animals hunted

Somehow might have brought cavemen good luck

Animals painted with blood, eggs, honey

have been there for generations;

in cave pictures — dark,

Five deer swimming

Shhhhh Look

Quiet

Directions

▸ Assign students to small collaborative groups. For younger students, assign a shorter poem. For older students, assign a longer poem.

▸ Provide students with an art reproduction, the upside-down triangle poem worksheet, and another sheet of paper for brainstorming words and phrases.

▸ Ask one student to be the recorder, the person who records words and phrases that other members of the collaborative group generate.

▸ After brainstorming for an ample amount of time, ask students to select one word on their brainstormed list that best describes the art object.

▸ This word should be entered on the blank at Line One.

▸ The second line contains two words. Students can choose to select two more "best words" from their brainstormed list or they can think of two other words that support or describe the first word. For example, if the first word was "modern," the next line might be "newly made." "Newly made" does not necessarily have to be included in the original brainstormed list.

▸ This process continues as each line becomes progressively one word longer than the previous line.

▸ What does this upside-down triangle poem tell you about the artwork that you might not otherwise have discovered?

▸ How does your poem tell about the artwork?

Suggested Works of Art

▸ Works that are narrative or show action

Upside-Down Triangle Poem

Title of the work of art _____

Name of the artist _____

_____ _____ _____ _____ _____ _____ _____ _____

Line 8

_____ _____ _____ _____ _____ _____ _____

Line 7

_____ _____ _____ _____ _____ _____

Line 6

_____ _____ _____ _____ _____

Line 5

_____ _____ _____ _____

Line 4

_____ _____ _____

Line 3

_____ _____

Line 2

_____

Line 1

W Poem

Interviewing an Artist

Letters: Formal and Informal

Venn Diagram

Classificatory Persuasive

Fact and Opinion

Acrostic Poems

Cinquain

Haiku

Upside-Down Triangle Poem

W Poem

Photo by Nancy Walkup.

W Poem

W poems are similar to the interview format because, like the interview, questions related to who, what, when, where, and why are explored. Unlike the interview format, however, students generate statements about each of these topics and then write a poem (rhyming or nonrhyming) about a work of art.

This is an example of a W poem written by a fourth-grade student about *Escher Bowl*, a tessellation by Jim McNeill:

> Football players
>
> Pushing and shoving
>
> Across the green field
>
> Playoff day…
>
> We want to win!

Directions

▸ Distribute an art reproduction and a W Poem worksheet to each student.

▸ Ask students to thoughtfully observe the work of art and then answer the questions on the worksheet.

▸ Answers should be derived from clues found in the art reproduction.

▸ After all answers are written, use the answers to create a W poem.

▸ The lines of the poem can use single words, short phrases, or complete sentences but should *not* use the words who, what, where, when, or why.

Suggested Works of Art

▸ Works that include characters, a sense of place and time, and action

W Poem

Title of the work of art _____

Look carefully at the work of art and then answer these questions:

Who is the subject? _____

What has happened? _____

Where did it happen? _____

When did it happen? _____

Why did it happen? _____

Now select words or phrases from your answers to create a poem that tells who, what, where, when, and why. Do *not* use the words who, what, where, when, and why in your poem. Use the lines below to write your final draft.

_____

_____

_____

_____

_____

Chapter 4
Art and Mathematics

"*My picture is no higher math. That I cannot state this more precisely is caused by my lack in mathematical training, I suppose. That is actually what is absorbing about my position as regards mathematics: our realms touch each other but do not overlap. I regret that!*"

— M. C. Escher, 1958

Art and Mathematics

Artists from different times and cultures have been fascinated by mathematical concepts and have used them to create unique works of art. From Islamic tile designs to rose windows in Medieval cathedrals, from Amish quilts to nonobjective paintings by Victor Vasarely, and from M. C. Escher's tessellations to Buckminster Fuller's geodesic domes, mathematical concepts have enthralled artists and architects. For all practical purposes, it is almost impossible to separate the artistic and mathematical concepts in such works.

There are particular mathematical concepts that may best be learned through experiences in art that directly correlate with math. Connections between art and math should be natural, logical, and meaningful and never forced or trivialized. For instance, counting the number of objects in an artwork is not a significant art or math activity. Artworks would be better served through investigations of the math concepts artists have deliberately chosen to incorporate in their work.

By combining art and mathematics, students are provided opportunities to solve problems creatively and develop spatial understanding through the exploration of geometry in two and three dimensions. In addition, students are afforded experiences to understand number, measurement, and pattern concepts, use manipulatives and representations, work collaboratively, and make further interdisciplinary connections through writing about art and math.

Art and Mathematics

Problem-Solving

Significant art and math activities present opportunities for students to develop and apply problem-solving skills. Such activities also encourage curiosity and creativity and help students understand the application of mathematics in real-life situations and the world around them. The use of manipulatives, objects that students can handle, move around, and place together, promotes student understanding of mathematics concepts and real-world applications. Manipulatives are intended for hands-on use by students. Commercial manipulatives are usually plastic or wooden shapes and forms that come in different sizes. Manipulatives are useful for demonstrating concepts, but by making art, students can create their own manipulatives.

Geometry

Geometry offers the most obvious connection between art and mathematics. Both involve drawing, the use of shapes and forms, an understanding of spatial concepts, geometry in two- and three-dimensions, measurement, estimation, and pattern. Many such math concepts find expression in art through the artist's use of the elements of art and principles of design in the composition of an artwork. Concepts of line, shape, form, pattern, symmetry, scale, and proportion, form the building blocks of art and parallel similar meanings in mathematics.

To learn geometric concepts, students need to investigate, experiment with, and explore the world of geometry through hands-on activities and everyday situations. For example, folding two-dimensional shapes into three-dimensional forms promotes the development of spatial sense. The creation of tessellation patterns made with congruent tiles or mosaics is another example of a significant experience that promotes understanding in both art and math.

Through other activities that combine art and mathematics concepts, students can explore bilateral and radial symmetry; practice using rulers, straight edges, protractors, and/or compasses; practice measurement and estimation; and create complex patterns based on geometric shapes and forms.

Photo by Nancy Walkup.

Vocabulary

It is beneficial for the art and mathematics teachers to learn and use the vocabulary for both subjects with their students. It is confusing for students to hear two different terms for the same concepts. For example, a two-dimensional shape, an art term, is called a plane figure in math. A three-dimensional form, again an art term, is called a space or solid figure in math. Concepts will be more meaningful if students use and understand the relationships for vocabulary for both art and math. Refer to the vocabulary list that follows for further examples of correlated terms.

Computers, Art, and Mathematics

Educational computer software for student use is becoming increasingly available. Painting and drawing programs and specialized software such as *Tesselmania! Deluxe* can engage students in problem-solving strategies in geometry, measurement, fractions, decimals, and other mathematical concepts while creating works of art on a computer. Encourage students to create original designs with software rather than using "prepackaged" patterns or images. Students can also use the Internet for research on art and math concepts.

Working Collaboratively

Small group or entire class collaborations are beneficial to help students understand the necessity of working well together and feel proud of their contributions to the group. Classroom paper quilts and painted murals are just two examples of art and mathematics projects that promote collaboration.

Art, Math, and Writing

Incorporating writing with art and mathematics activities provides experiences with an additional communication skill. Students can keep journals, describe problems and solutions in sentence form, detail the steps of a process, and write their own stories about art and math.

Vocabulary

Circumference: the perimeter of a circle

Congruent: exactly the same in size and shape

Diameter: the length of a line that passes through the center of a circle

Equilateral triangle: a triangle with three sides the same length

Form/Space or solid figure: a three-dimensional figure

Isosceles triangle: a triangle with at least two sides the same length

Line segment: the portion of a line between any two points on the line

Manipulatives: objects that students can handle, move around, and place together; commercially- or student-made; commercial manipulatives are usually plastic or wooden shapes and forms that come in different sizes

Parallelogram: a figure with two pairs of parallel sides and two pairs of sides the same length

Polygon: a closed plane figure bounded by three or more line segments

Quadrilateral: a four-sided polygon

Radius: a line segment from the center of a circle to the circumference

Rectangle: a polygon with two pairs of sides the same length and all right angles

Regular polygon: polyhedron with all sides congruent and all angles congruent, such as pentagon, hexagon, and octagon

Rhombus: a diamond-shaped parallelogram with four equal sides; an oblique-angled equilateral parallelogram

Scalene triangle: a triangle in which no sides are the same

Shape/plane figure: a two-dimensional figure in which all points lie in the same plane

Square: a polygon with four sides the same length and four right angles

Symmetry: exact correspondence of form on opposite sides of a dividing line

Tessellation: a congruent shape repeated in a pattern

Tetrahedron: a space or solid figure bounded by four triangles

Three-dimensional: having three-dimensions—height, width, and depth

Triangle: a figure bounded by three lines containing three angles

Two-dimensional: having only two dimensions, such as height and width

Resources

Brown, Kurt. *Poems about Science and Mathematics.* Milkweed Editions, 1998.

The Oxford Treasury of Time Poems. Oxford University Press, 1998.

Shapiro, Norman. *Geometry through Art.* Available http://forum.swathmore.edu/ ~sarah/shapiro/

Geometric Shapes and Forms

Geometric Shapes and Forms

Symmetry

Proportion

Op Art and Optical Illusions

Tessellations and other Congruent Shapes

Perspective

Graphing Responses to Works of Art

Geodesic Structures and Tetrahedrons

Origami

Geometric Shapes and Forms

To learn geometric concepts, students need to investigate, experiment with, and explore the world of geometry through hands-on activities and everyday situations. Students of all ages can work with geometric shapes and forms while using both art and mathematics terms when discussing geometric concepts. For instance, shapes are called plane figures and forms are called space figures or solid figures in mathematics. Consult the vocabulary list for further definitions.

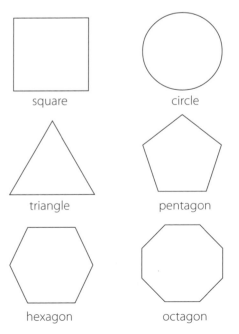

square   circle

triangle   pentagon

hexagon   octagon

Activities

▶ Use math manipulatives (plastic geometric shapes) to explore combining geometric shapes to form quilt-like patterns.

▶ Look for geometric designs in functional items from different cultures. Discuss why people are drawn to geometric designs.

▶ Use geometric shapes in drawing, painting, or collage.

▶ Make colored construction paper quilt blocks based on 4-, 9-, or 16-square designs, then combine them to make a class quilt. To provide unity in the class quilt, use the same color for all the background squares and limit other colors to three or four (for example, use a black or white background and the primary colors of red, yellow, and blue for the geometric design).

▶ Create geometric, quilt-like designs on large-scale grid paper, experimenting with color, pattern, texture, and design. Use a ruler and pencil to accurately measure and draw grids or use teacher-prepared grids (sized according to ability levels). Use different colored pencils or markers and experiment with rotation and reflection. Adjacent shapes can be made the same color to create other shapes.

▶ Make paper weavings using contrasting colors and strips of construction paper.

▶ Make yarn weavings with geometric designs.

▶ In a journal, describe in sequence the steps used to make a simple geometric quilt block.

▶ Create elaborate quilt-like designs on half- or quarter-inch grid paper or a computer painting or drawing program, experimenting with color, pattern, texture, and design (real quilters often work this way).

▶ Plan elaborate geometric quilt designs on grid paper in colored pencil or marker. Translate the grid paper design to a large-scale acrylic painting.

▶ Use traditional quilt names to inspire geometric designs that are visual puns. Some names to consider include baseball, bird's nest, bow tie, box quilt, broken dishes, card trick, castle wall, city square, double arrow, flying saucer, goose tracks, Jack-in-the-box, shooting star, toad in a puddle, wheel of fortune, and wild goose chase.

Geometric Shapes and Forms

▸ Research regional names for quilt patterns, then create and name an original geometric design that represents your state or region.

▸ An album quilt is one in which a different person contributes each square. They are often made to commemorate a special occasion. Make a class album quilt using fabric and traditional quilting techniques such as piecing and applique.

▸ Compare and contrast an Amish quilt with a nonobjective contemporary work of art.

▸ Dicuss whether or not (and why) it is appropriate to place a quilt in a museum.

Suggested Artworks and Artists

▸ Amish quilts

▸ American colonial patchwork quilts

▸ Navajo and other geometric-patterned weavings

▸ Sol Lewitt

▸ Faith Ringgold

▸ Jim McNeill, *Escher Bowl*

▸ Victor Vasarely, *Gestalt-Zoeld*

▸ Chuck Close

Activity: Collaborative Paper Quilt

Traditional American quilts are largely based on precisely premeasured, repeating symmetrical blocks. Though blocks in the class quilt will vary in design, they should all be the same size so that they may be pieced and fit together for the final quilt. Begin with a 9-in. or 12-in. construction paper square as the background. Measure and cut squares and triangles from other colors of same-size squares. Arrange the complete geometric design on the background square before gluing in place. When all the squares are complete, lay them on a large piece of butcher or other strong paper on the floor in an open area of the classroom. Place the finished blocks edge to edge or separate by paper strip borders. Glue in place and display. Paper quilts may also be made by gluing fabric shapes on paper with diluted white glue or using patterned wallpaper or wrapping paper for "piecing."

Photo by Nancy Walkup.

Activity: Paper Weaving

Make square paper weavings using contrasting colors such as pairs of complementary colors—red/green, blue/orange, or yellow/purple. To make an individual weaving, begin by folding a 9 x 9-in. colored construction paper square in half. With a ruler aligned on the open end of the folded paper, mark off a one-inch strip with a pencil. With the paper still folded, draw parallel lines down from the horizontal line to the fold. Lines may be straight, zigzag, wavy, or a combination, but draw lines at least one inch apart. Cut on the drawn lines up to the horizontal line, but not past it. Open up the paper

and flatten it. This is the paper loom in which the cut strips form the warp. On a second 9 x 9-in. piece of construction paper (use a different color), draw parallel lines all the way across the width of the paper. Cut these strips completely apart—these will form the weft. Weave the weft strips into the warp, over and under, in an alternating fashion in the order in which they were cut, pushing them close together on the loom. Weave in as many strips as possible, then glue down the ends of the strips on both sides. Arrange the finished squares from the class into a quilt-like format. Weavings could also be rectangular in shape.

Symmetry

Geometric Shapes and Forms

Symmetry

Proportion

Op Art and Optical Illusions

Tessellations and other Congruent Shapes

Perspective

Graphing Responses to Works of Art

Geodesic Structures and Tetrahedrons

Origami

Symmetry

The concept of symmetry or symmetrical balance is fundamental to art, math, and science. Symmetry is a type of balance in which the two halves of a whole are each other's mirror images. The parts on either side of a centerline are exactly (in art, math, and science) or nearly the same (as in approximate symmetry in art). A centerline, called the line of symmetry, divides an image or object in half so that one side mirrors the other. This concept is also called reflectional or mirror symmetry in math and bilateral symmetry in science. In radial balance, a form of symmetrical balance, the elements of a composition radiate from a central axis in a regularly repeating pattern. Another type of balance is called asymmetrical balance, in which the two sides of a composition are different but visually balanced, visually equal without being identical.

Activities

▶ Find photographs of living things with bilateral symmetry and use them as guides for accuracy. Make colored construction paper creatures, such as figures of insects, amphibians, mammals, or people. Fold rectangles of construction paper in half along the line of symmetry and draw half of a creature against the fold, checking that the backbone or body is placed against the folded line. Carefully cut apart the half-creature without cutting on the fold or cutting the two halves apart. Open up the paper, and then use scrap paper and crayons or markers to add symmetrical details and decorative features.

▶ Use the above procedure to make elaborate nonobjective designs.

▶ Create an intricate weaving that is symmetrical.

▶ Compare and contrast symmetry in masks from around the world.

▶ Make a symmetrical mask.

▶ Create portraits that exhibit symmetrical faces and/or bodies (see diagrams under proportion).

▶ Discuss whether (and why) masks belong in art, anthropology, or natural history museums.

Suggested Artworks and Artists

▶ M. C. Escher

▶ Judy Chicago

▶ Robert Indiana

Resources

Hargittai, Istvan, and Magdolna Hargittai. *Symmetry: A Unifying Concept.* Shelter Publications, 1996.

Holden, Alan. *Shapes, Space, and Symmetry;* Dover, 1991.

Rosen, Joe. *Symmetry Discovered : Concepts and Applications in Nature and Science.* Dover, 1998.

Stevens, Peter S., and C. Peter Smith. *Handbook of Regular Patterns: An Introduction to Symmetry in Two Dimensions.* MIT Press, 1992.

Radial Symmetry

Radial symmetry or balance is a form of symmetrical balance in which the elements of a composition radiate from a central axis in a regular repeating pattern. Images or objects that are symmetrical can be divided in half with a line of symmetry, an imaginary line that divides an image so that one side is a mirror of the other. The line of symmetry in a radial design can cross the central axis in infinite number. Radial symmetry designs are sometimes called mandalas. Radial symmetry can be found in living things (flowers, starfish, jellyfish), natural objects (crystals, snowflakes), human-made objects (kaleidoscopes, hubcaps and wheels, face of a clock, pinwheel), and works of art.

In art and aesthetic expression, radial symmetry often takes the form of a mandala—a Sanskrit word that means "whole world" or "healing circle." It is visualized in Native American and Tibetan sand paintings, gothic rose windows, labyrinths, and other circular symbols of meditation, healing, and protection.

Activities

- Conduct a "treasure hunt" around the classroom and school to locate examples of radial symmetry. Bring other examples from home for display and discussion.

- To make a color pencil or marker radial design mandala, trace a 9-in. circle pattern on white drawing paper, then divide it into quarters using a wedge-shaped pattern, then add designs with markers, colored pencils, or crayons. Complete one wedge first, and then repeat the design in each quarter of the circle.

- Cut snowflake-like designs from paper.

- Identify, display, and discuss real-life examples of radial symmetry, both from natural and human-made sources that use geometric shapes. Explore methods of accurately measuring circles to divide them into halves and fourths. Use different sizes of circle patterns and pencils, rulers, and scissors to investigate and predict the results of combining, subdividing, and changing shapes in radial symmetry designs. Create completed mandalas that use only geometric shapes.

- Research the use of radial symmetry in art from around the world. Find examples of mandalas and compare and contrast their use, especially focusing on their similarities.

- Make cut paper mandalas by tracing a 9-in. diameter circle on 10 x 10-in. white drawing paper or thin colored paper, using a teacher-made pattern or a large round lid. Cut out the traced circle, and then fold it in half, then quarters. Using scissors, cut out designs along both folded edges of the wedge; be careful not to cut away too much. Open and flatten the folded paper, and then glue the mandala onto another color of 10 x 10-in. paper. Using other colors of paper, cut shapes and glue them on the circle, repeating the same design in each wedge.

- To make a radial symmetry crayon resist, use a 9-in. circle pattern or large lid to trace a circle on white or manila drawing paper. Using estimation, draw a thick line with a bright colored crayon to divide the circle in half and draw a second line to divide the circle into quarters. Using only bright color crayons, draw line designs close together to cover the circle, repeating the same design and colors in each quarter. Use pressure on the crayons to make thick lines with heavy color, but do not fill in the entire circle. Leave some of the background paper showing between all crayoned lines. When the crayoned lines are complete, brush thin black tempera paint over the entire design. The thick layers of crayon will "resist" the paint so that the shiny, crayoned colors will contrast with the black matte background.

- Create an abstract design inspired by the design of automobile hubcaps and wheels.

- View and discuss examples of radial symmetry from natural sources and from different cultures, times, and artists. Design a complex mandala/radial symmetry design.

Symmetry

▸ Use a ruler, compass, and protractor to accurately measure and draw complex radial symmetry designs utilizing geometric shapes. Adjust the scale of the work according to the materials and designs chosen — works may range in size from very small and detailed to large and bold.

▸ Experiment with mirror symmetry through kaleidoscope designs. A kaleidoscope is an optical instrument—a tube that contains three mirrors placed at 60-degree angles to each other. When the kaleidoscope is held to the eye and turned, colored glass or similar materials at one end of the tube are reflected as symmetrical designs within a hexagon. Originally designed as a toy, the kaleidoscope was invented in 1816 by David Brewster. Try making a kaleidoscope or plan a design for one.

▸ Use computer software drawing or paint programs to create elaborate mandala designs from geometric shapes.

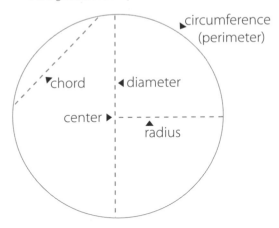

Suggested Artworks and Artists

▸ North Rose Window, Cathedral of Notre Dame, Paris, France

▸ Southwest Native American Pottery

Resources

Finkel, Norma, and Finkel, Leslie. *Kaleidoscope Designs and How to Create Them.* Mineola, NY: Dover Publications, 1980.

Kennedy, Joe, and Thomas, Diane. *Kaleidoscope Math.* Creative Publications, 1989.

Radial Symmetry Design

Using a 9-in. diameter circle pattern cut from tagboard, trace a circle on 12 x 12-in. white drawing paper, then set it aside. Choose a $\frac{1}{4}$ or $\frac{1}{6}$ wedge tagboard pattern and trace it to divide the 9-in. circle into quarters or sixths. Set this aside and then trace two of the wedges on $8\frac{1}{2}$ x 11-in. white copy paper. Use these "practice" wedges to plan a design.

Draw in pencil in each wedge an intricate line design that completely fills the space. Designs may be realistic, abstract or nonobjective, geometric or organic, but intricate designs work best when repeated through the radial symmetry of the mandala. After the drawing is complete, shade the back of the wedge with a pencil, then cut out the wedge.

Align the design wedge in the circle traced earlier and hold it in place with small pieces of masking tape. Trace over the design with a pencil to transfer it to the underlying paper. Repeat by moving the wedge and retracing the image until the circle is complete. Remove the wedge, then color the mandala with markers or colored pencils, repeating the same colors, values, and textures until the circle is complete.

Other options include the use of two different designs that are alternated around the circle, increasing the scale of the work by beginning with a larger circle, and creating very intricate designs using only black and white.

Radial Symmetry Design

Name _____

Class _____

Use this page to plan your radial symmetry design. You may sketch from one to four designs in the four sections of the circle to plan your design. When you have completed the design you want to use, lay a new piece of paper over your sketch and trace the outline of the circle. Transfer your chosen design by tracing it over in one quadrant, repeating the same process until your circle is complete. Color each quadrant exactly the same.

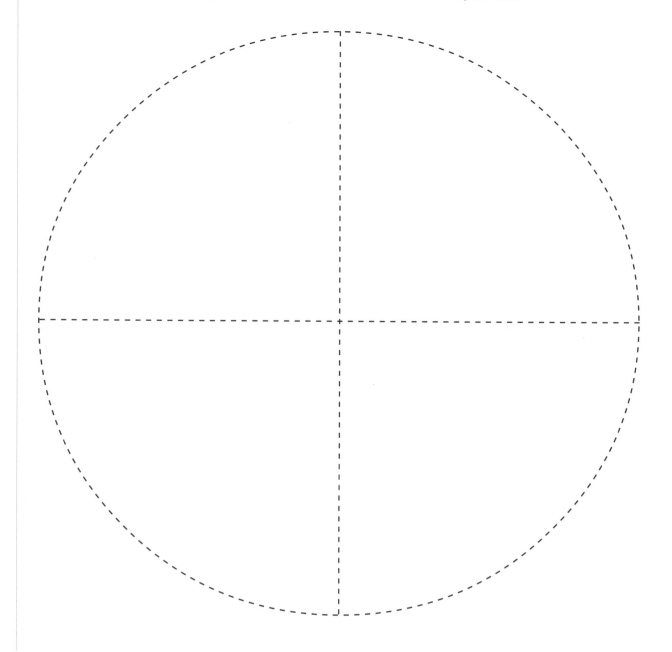

Symmetry

Proportion and the Golden Mean

In art, proportion is the principle of design concerned with the size relationships of parts of a composition to each other and to the whole. In mathematics, proportion is the ratio or relation of one part to another or to the whole with respect to size, quantity, or degree. During the Renaissance, mathematicians took special interest in how many objects in nature reflected mathematical principles. As they discovered connections, they developed mathematical ideas to help understand the relationship between math and nature. For example, the Golden Mean (also called Golden Ratio, Section, or Proportion) was used by many Renaissance artists and architects who learned about it from studying the ancient Greeks. It describes a proportion in which the ratio of the whole to the larger part is the same as the ratio of the larger part to the smaller, a ratio of 1 to 1.62, or about one-third to two-thirds. The Golden Mean is seen as aesthetically or visually pleasing to human beings. Such proportions can be found in the growth patterns in shells and fern fronds. Artists have used the Golden Mean to plan the compositions of their works. Leonardo da Vinci superimposed the proportions of the human body over geometric forms—a circle in a square—to simplify the measurements of the body in his *Vitruvian Man* drawing.

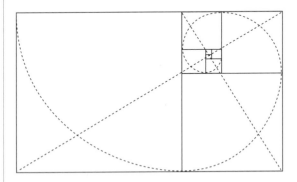

Activities

▶ The ancient Greeks considered the Golden Mean to be the ideal proportion for the human figure. If the average human figure is divided at the navel, the resulting measurements have a ratio of 1 to 1.62. Ideals of human proportion vary over time and cultures. The most recent ideal uses the measurement of the head from the top of the skull to the bottom of the chin to determine the proportions of the figure. The average adult is seven heads tall, but individual proportions will vary depending on the size, shape, and age of the subject. Children vary from five to six heads tall; infants may be only three heads tall and have heads proportionately larger to the rest of the body. Try drawing a figure using these guidelines.

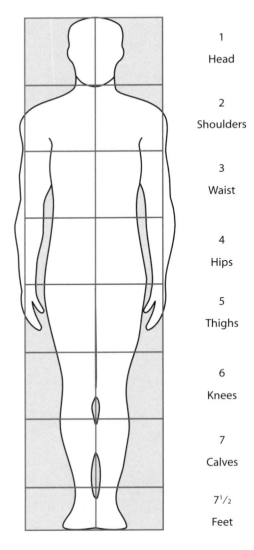

1
Head

2
Shoulders

3
Waist

4
Hips

5
Thighs

6
Knees

7
Calves

7¹/₂
Feet

Symmetry

Photo by Nancy Walkup.

▶ Create a portrait following these guidelines. Try both forward-facing and profile portraits.

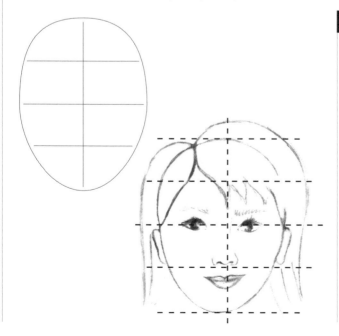

▶ Use a grid to enlarge an image without losing its proper proportions. Begin by drawing a grid of one-inch squares on an image such as an art postcard or a photograph brought from home. Decide what scale to use to enlarge the image—for example, a ratio of four to one would mean your final image would be four times larger than the original. Draw this larger grid on drawing paper, then copy the small squares into the bigger squares to make a larger image. Complete the picture with crayons, paints, or markers, then display the two images side-by-side.

▶ Adapt the grid method for use with a group of students. Grid squares with lines on a large art reproduction. Number the back of the image in each square, then cut the print apart. Give each student one square to enlarge and assign the ratio you prefer ($\frac{1}{2}$ or $\frac{1}{3}$, depending on the size of the reproduction). When all the squares are complete, put together the pieces of the puzzle and display (the numbers on the back will help in assembly).

Suggested Artworks and Artists

▶ Leonardo da Vinci, *Vitruvian Man*

▶ Chuck Close

Resources

Chuck Close: A Portrait in Progress. Home Vision Arts, 4411 N. Ravenswood Ave., Third Floor, Chicago, IL 60640-5803, video.

Dunlap. R. A. *The Golden Ratio and Fibonacci Numbers.* World Scientific, 1998.

Greenberg, Jan, and Sandra Jordan. *Chuck Close Up Close.* New York: DK Publishing, 1998.

Herz-Fischles, Roger. *Mathematical History of the Golden Number.* Dover Publications, 1998.

McIntosh, Stephen. *The Golden Mean Book & Caliper Set.* Now and Zen, 1997.

Runion, Garth E. *Golden Section.* Dale Seymour Publications, 1990.

Op Art and Optical Illusions

Geometric Shapes and Forms

Symmetry

Proportion

Op Art and Optical Illusions

Tessellations and other Congruent Shapes

Perspective

Graphing Responses to Works of Art

Geodesic Structures and Tetrahedrons

Origami

Op Art and Optical Illusions

Op or Optical Art developed in the 1960s in Europe and the United States as an alternative to the classic representation of perspective in two-dimensional artwork. It customarily creates the illusion of three-dimensional space on a two-dimensional plane. Op art attempts not only to trick the viewer's eye into seeing movement, but also attempts to convey the actual feeling of movement to the viewer's senses. Quite often Op Art images appear to be made by computer rather than by hand. This is because the artist must be exactingly precise with the lines, shapes, and colors of the images. With the intent of tricking the viewer's eye, it is necessary that the image be as perfect as possible. Even the smallest error (such as misplaced color or a line drawn the wrong width) could ruin the visual effect.

Activities

▶ Compare and contrast Op Art designs from different artists.

▶ Use math manipulatives to explore the creation of patterns with combinations of congruent shapes. Use mirrors to examine how the appearance of shapes can be changed through reflection.

▶ Use half- or one-inch grid paper for planning optical designs. Enlarge completed designs using a grid method, then paint as desired. Use dark and light colors, lines, textures, and/or patterns to create optical illusions such as the illusion of depth.

▶ Use a distorted grid rather than a mathematical one as the basis for a design. Distort both horizontal and vertical lines, then apply color or only black and white.

▶ Explore combining congruent shapes to create new shapes; for example, joining two equilateral triangles makes a rhombus or diamond shape. Use teacher-made rhombus or triangle templates to trace and cut out congruent shapes from colored construction paper. Cut out a number of different colored shapes and arrange them in a pleasing design on a large piece of drawing or construction paper. Experiment with leaving some spaces open, setting pieces side by side, or leaving a narrow gap between each shape to allow the background paper to "outline" the shapes.

▶ Use large-scale grid paper to create designs using only squares, diamonds, and triangles. Add color with markers or pencils. As a variation, lay the grid paper under white copy paper as a guideline for planning designs.

▶ Use computer draw and/or paint programs to create Op Art designs.

▶ Use commercial half-inch grid paper or make your own to use for planning optical illusion designs (to use the grid paper as a guide, lay it underneath a clean sheet of copy paper). Outline your design in pencil, then use markers or colored pencils to fill in color. The illusion of depth can be created through the selective use of diagonal lines and dark and light colors. Dark colors will appear to recede, while light colors will seem to come forward. Enlarge the completed design to the desired scale, using the grid method on a large board or canvas, then paint as desired. Use dark and light colors, lines and textures, and/or patterns to create optical illusions such as the illusion of depth.

▶ Use a distorted grid rather than a mathematical one as the basis for a design. Distort both horizontal and vertical lines, then apply color or only black and white.

▶ Limit the colors in an Op Art design to a pair of complementary colors—blue/orange, red/green, or yellow/violet.

▶ Experiment with figure/ground relationships and positive/negative space.

▶ Compare and contrast Op Art with linear perspective (refer to pages 60-61 of this book).

Op Art and Optical Illusions

Suggested Artists

▶ Victor Vaserely

▶ Bridget Riley

▶ Sandor Kara

▶ Rene Parola

▶ Jim McNeill

Resources

Baum, Arline, and Joseph Baum. *Opt: An Illusionary Tale.* Viking Press, 1989.

Jennings, Terry. *101 Amazing Optical Illusions: Fantastic Visual Tricks.* Sterling Publications, 1998.

Simon, Seymour. *The Optical Illusion Book.* William Morrow, 1984.

Sturgis, Alexander. *Optical Illusions in Art.* New York: Sterling Publishing Co., Inc., 1996.

Tessellations and Other Congruent Shapes

Geometric Shapes and Forms

Symmetry

Proportion

Op Art and Optical Illusions

Tessellations and other Congruent Shapes

Perspective

Graphing Responses to Works of Art

Geodesic Structures and Tetrahedrons

Origami

Blueblood, Jim McNeill.

Tessellations and Other Congruent Shapes

A tessellation is a pattern made using congruent shapes—shapes that are exactly the same in size and outline. The simplest tessellations are made using a regular polygon (a geometric shape with all sides and angles alike) such as a square, triangle, rhombus (diamond), pentagon (5 sides), hexagon (6), or octagon (8) and tracing it repeatedly, side-by-side. Three types of symmetry found in tessellations are translational, rotational, and reflectional (mirror).

An example of a real-life tessellation would be a floor made from tiles. More interesting tessellations are made by making a template of a more complex tessellating shape and sliding, turning, or reversing it in a regular pattern. The pattern is repeated in a vertical or horizontal format until the desired design is achieved. Details can then be added. More complex tessellations are created by using more than one shape or details and color, but all tessellations appear to fit together like the pieces of a puzzle.

The History of Tessellations

Tessellations have been found that date from as early as 4000 BC and are evident even today in Moorish architecture in Spain and Islamic architecture in the Middle East. The creators of these tessellations were (and still are) constrained by their religion from using representational images. No images of people, animals, or other recognizable subjects may be used, but Islamic artists have developed amazingly elaborate and beautiful geometric, arabesque, floral, and calligraphic designs for tiled mosaic floors, walls, and architecture. Many of these designs form tessellations.

The 20th century artist most recognized for his tessellated images is Maurits Cornelius Escher (M.C. Escher). Escher, a Dutch graphic artist who lived from 1898-1972, worked primarily with woodblock and lithographic printmaking processes. His images include intricate optical illusions, impossible structures, and complex tessellations. A contemporary tessellation artist whose work can be found on the Internet is Jim McNeill.

Tessellations and Other Congruent Shapes

Activities

▸ Compare and contrast artworks based on tessellations.

▸ Identify examples of congruent shapes found both in natural and human-made environments. Look for squares, equilateral triangles, pentagons, hexagons, and octagons. Bring examples of tessellations and congruent shapes to class for display and discussion.

▸ Use math manipulatives to explore the creation of patterns with combinations of congruent shapes. Use mirrors to examine how the appearance of shapes can be changed through reflection.

▸ Use templates of equilateral triangles and diamonds to draw and cut shapes from colored construction paper. Arrange the shapes as desired on a large background piece of paper, and then glue in place.

▸ Use large-scale grid paper to create designs using only squares, diamonds, and triangles. Add color with markers or pencils.

▸ Print repeating patterns using stamps of geometric shapes made from erasers or Model Magic modeling material.

▸ Tessellation activities may be varied from simple to complex. Even young children can work with the basic shapes of squares and equilateral triangles; upper elementary students can make tessellations based on translations, a transformation using a slide.

▸ Complete one to three tessellations, each with the simple geometric shapes of a square, an equilateral triangle, and a hexagon. Use the patterns provided in this book or measure and cut them out. Each form requires a different use of the pattern; the square fits evenly side by side, the triangle is flipped every time it is traced, and the hexagon slides up and down to fit.

▸ Cut congruent shapes from two colors of colored construction paper and alternate them in repeating patterns over a background color. Glue in place when the arrangement is complete.

▸ Make congruent square or triangular clay tiles and embellish them by adding texture and/or color by painting or glazing. Assemble completed tiles for a permanent mural and install in the office, library, or other place in the school.

▸ Make computer-generated tessellations with paint and/or draw computer programs or special software such as *TesselMania! Deluxe*.

▸ Conduct research on the Internet to learn more about the connections between art, mathematics, and tessellations.

▸ Find pictures that show mirror or reflectional symmetry, such as architecture or sculptures that are positioned with a reflecting pool such as the Jefferson Memorial or Washington Memorial.

▸ Create complex, original tessellation tiles using techniques that involve translation (a transformation using a slide) or rotation (a transformation that turns a figure about a point in a plane). (See pages 58-59)

▸ Write down the steps taken to make a tessellation and the reasons for choosing your design. Display the writings along with the completed tessellations.

▸ Make a number of congruent clay tiles and assemble them with grout after they are fired and glazed.

Suggested Artworks and Artists

▸ M.C. Escher, *Reptiles*

▸ Jim McNeill, *Escher Bowl*

▸ The Alhambra, Granada, Spain

Resources

Beyer, Jinny. *Designing Tessellations: The Secrets of Interlocking Patterns*. Contemporary Books, 1999.

The Fantastic World of M.C. Escher. Atlas Video, 1994, video.

Seymour, Dale, and Jill Britton. *Introduction to Tessellations*. Palo Alto, California: Dale Seymour Publications, 1989.

Tessellations: How to Create Them. Crystal Productions, 1999, video.

Translation Tessellation

A translation is a transformation of a tessellation that involves a slide (or glide) of a figure without rotation. To create a simple translation, use a 3-in. square cut from an index card or similar weight paper as a template. Number the corners of the template 1, 2, 3, and 4, beginning with 1 in the upper left side. Next, draw a simple wavy or zigzag line from corner 1 to corner 2. Carefully cut along this line to separate the square into two pieces. Slide the shape that is cut free down to the opposite and outside edge of the square. Tape it in place, matching the two straight edges of the two shapes. The shapes should fit together side-by-side, with no overlap.

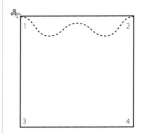 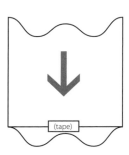

Next draw a wavy or zigzag line from corner 1 to corner 4, then cut along the line. Slide this cut shape to the right and outside edge of the square, and then align the straight edges and tape the two pieces together. This process creates a tessellation "tile" or pattern piece. When the same shape is repeatedly traced without leaving gaps between the shapes, a repeat pattern is created which is congruent—all the shapes in the pattern are exactly alike. (Once the basic process is understood, students may want to practice making several tiles before choosing one to use for a completed tessellation design.)

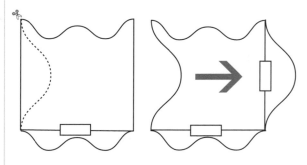

Set the template aside and use a ruler and pencil to measure and draw a 3-in. grid on a 12 x 18-in. piece of colored construction or drawing paper. Accuracy is very important here so this step may take some time, but the activity is beneficial for practicing measurement skills.

To fill a paper with the tessellated pattern, begin by tracing in pencil the perimeter of the "tile" next to both edges on the upper left corner of the previously gridded paper. Fit the tessellation pattern next to the first tracing and trace again. Repeat this process, moving from left to right and top to bottom, until the paper is filled with congruent shapes. Parts of the shape may seem to run off the paper and that is natural. A tessellating plane is infinite, so it will never have a finished, straight edge. Look carefully at the design created to see if it suggests a face, animal, or object. If desired, add details such as eyes, a nose, mouth, or other feature, repeating the same process in all the tiles. Use tempera paints or colored markers to complete the tessellation. Each tile may be colored the same way or two designs can be alternated to create more variety in the work.

Designing a tessellation: The sides of a tile may be modified by drawing random curves or lines, then interpreting the resulting shape by adding details to its interior. Another, more difficult, method is to have a specific object in mind and modify the sides of the tile until it resembles the desired object.

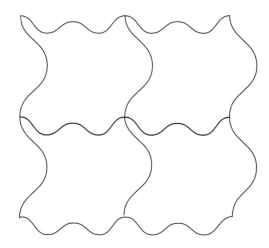

Rotation Tessellation

A rotation is a tessellation that turns a figure about a point on a plane. In this approach, again start by tracing a 3-in. square template and numbering the corners 1, 2, 3, and 4. Draw a line from corner 1 to corner 2 and cut the square apart along the drawn line. Rotate the cut shape counterclockwise around the upper right corner of the template and tape in place. Next draw a line from corner 1 to corner 4, then cut along the line. Rotate this cut shape clockwise around the lower left corner to the bottom edge of the template and tape into place.

Set template aside and use a ruler and pencil to measure and draw a 3-in. grid on a 12 x 18-in. piece of colored construction or drawing paper. Accuracy is very important here so this step may take some time, but the activity is beneficial for practicing measurement skills.

Begin with the template in the middle of the paper. Trace the tile, and then hold the tile at its top right corner and rotate it 90° counterclockwise. Align it with the grid lines and trace. Continue the rotation with the tile. Repeat the same procedure to fill the paper, then complete as desired.

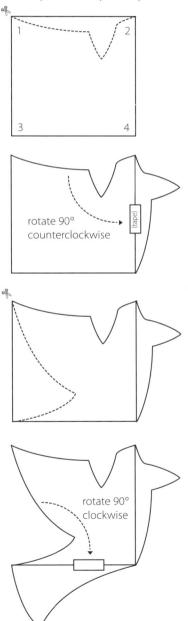

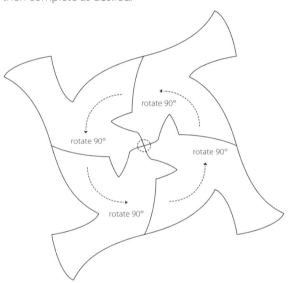

Whirlybird, Jim McNeill.

Perspective

Geometric Shapes and Forms

Symmetry

Proportion

Op Art and Optical Illusions

Tessellations and other Congruent Shapes

Perspective

Graphing Responses to Works of Art

Geodesic Structures and Tetrahedrons

Origami

Illustration by Gerald Brommer.

Perspective

Perspective is the representation of three-dimensional objects in space on a two-dimensional, flat surface. The system of drawing called perspective was developed by Renaissance artists Brunelleschi, Alberti, Uccello, and Piero della Francesca and grew from the artists' fascination with mathematics. The simplest form of perspective drawing is called linear perspective, a system that allows artists to trick the eye into seeing depth on a flat surface. Linear perspective uses sets of implied lines called convergence or

orthogonal lines that move closer together in the distance until they merge at an imaginary vanishing point on the horizon. One-point perspective uses lines that lead to a single vanishing point, while two-point perspective uses lines that lead to two different vanishing points. Two-point perspective appears more similar to human vision than does one-point. Perspective drawings and paintings represent the impression of distance and relative size as perceived by the human eye. Forms that are far away seem smaller to the eye than those that are close up.

There are three major viewpoints used for perspective drawing. The directions for one- and two-point perspective here given represent an eye level viewpoint, placing the horizon line at eye level. A high viewpoint (bird's eye) will show a horizon high on the page, while a low viewpoint (worm's eye) has a low horizon.

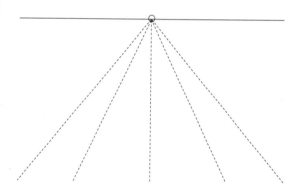

One-Point Perspective

With a pencil and ruler, draw a horizontal line all the way across a paper at the desired eye level. Draw a dot for the vanishing point near the middle of the line. Use the horizon line and the vanishing point as guides for the perspective drawing. The front edge or plane of each solid is parallel to the edge of the paper. The top, sides, and bottom edges of planes are drawn along lines that converge at the vanishing point. In one-point perspective, all vertical and horizontal lines stay the same and all planes are perpendicular or parallel to the horizon. Only lines that are moving from or toward the vanishing point seem to recede to the horizon at the vanishing point. Draw horizontal and vertical lines first, and then lightly draw the convergence lines. Use the horizon line and vanishing point to guide the development of the drawing. Erase the convergence lines when they are no longer needed.

Perspective

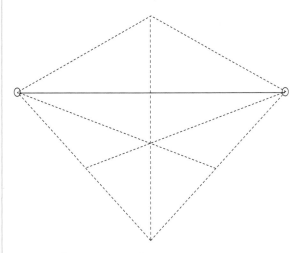

Two-Point Perspective

With a pencil and ruler, draw a horizontal line all the way across a paper at the desired eye level. Draw a dot for each of two vanishing points on the horizon line at both sides of the paper. Use the horizon line and vanishing points to guide the development of the drawing. All vertical lines remain vertical but parallel lines seem to recede to the same vanishing point. Both front and side planes seem to recede in depth. Draw vertical lines first, and then lightly draw the convergence lines. Use the horizon line and vanishing points to guide the development of the drawing, drawing a cube for your first effort. Erase the convergence lines when they are no longer needed. Two-point perspective appears more similar to human vision than does one-point perspective.

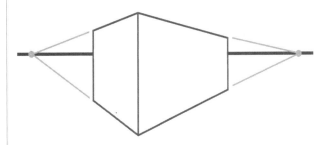

Activities

▶ Younger students can be introduced to perspective by first working with using other methods to suggest the concepts of near and far away. Overlap and the relative size and placement of objects on a page can demonstrate distance (objects larger and lower on the picture plane look closer; objects smaller and higher on the picture plane look smaller).

▶ Create a drawing with one-point perspective.

▶ Create a drawing with two-point perspective.

▶ Compare and contrast the use of perspective by several artists.

▶ Investigate atmospheric perspective.

▶ Compare and contrast linear perspective with other systems for depicting space, especially with work by Australian aborigines and Japanese printmakers.

Suggested Artworks and Artists

▶ Filippo Brunelleschi, Dome of the Cathedral of Florence, 1417-1436, lantern completed 1471

▶ Leon Battista Alberti, *The Deluge*, c. 1448

▶ Piero della Francesca, *View of an Ideal City*, 1460

▶ Raphael, *The School of Athens*, 1509-1511

▶ Leonardo da Vinci, *The Last Supper*, 1495

Resources

Brommer, Gerald, *Basic Perspective Drawing,* video. Crystal Productions, 1996.

Masters of Illusion, video, National Gallery of Art

Smith, Ray, and Michael Wright. *DK Art School: An Introduction to Perspective.* DK Publishing, 1995.

Stanley, Diane. *Leonardo da Vinci.* William Morrow and Company, 1996.

Striegel, Oliver. *Drawing in Perspective.* Sterling Publications, 1998.

Graphing Responses to Works of Art

Graphing provides a method to compare and contrast student responses to art. The graph on this page is designed for use with five works of art.

▸ Use large reproductions for this activity. Place students in five collaborative groups and display the five reproductions. Give each student a set of two or three tokens (photocopy the following page). Encourage students to walk around and look at the images without consulting anyone else. Ask students to vote by placing their tokens upside down by the chosen image, and then return to their groups. As there is one image per group, each group sorts the votes for the image at their desk and tabulates the responses. One person from each group writes the title of the work of art and the artist's name on the worksheet (photocopy from the following page). Along the bottom axis of the graph, write in the various categories chosen. Share group responses with the class.

▸ Use other categories as desired, perhaps types of art or themes.

▸ Have students line up in rows according to their responses to form a living bar graph.

Worksheet for Student Groups

Instructions: Appoint a recorder for your group, then use the tokens given to your group by the teacher to mark your responses to the artworks used for this activity. Return to your group and tally the responses left for the artwork at your table. The recorder should indicate on the graph below the number of response cards given for each of the categories. Share responses in a class discussion.

Title of Artwork: _____

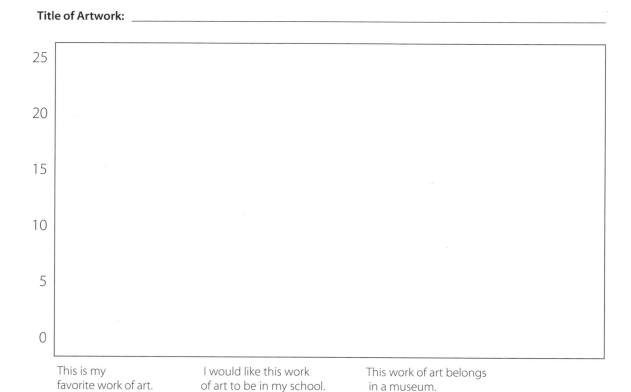

25

20

15

10

5

0

| This is my favorite work of art. | I would like this work of art to be in my school. | This work of art belongs in a museum. |

Graphing Responses to Works of Art

This is my favorite work of art.	I would like this work of art to be in my school.	This work of art belongs in a museum.
This is my favorite work of art.	I would like this work of art to be in my school.	This work of art belongs in a museum.
This is my favorite work of art.	I would like this work of art to be in my school.	This work of art belongs in a museum.
This is my favorite work of art.	I would like this work of art to be in my school.	This work of art belongs in a museum.
This is my favorite work of art.	I would like this work of art to be in my school.	This work of art belongs in a museum.
This is my favorite work of art.	I would like this work of art to be in my school.	This work of art belongs in a museum.
This is my favorite work of art.	I would like this work of art to be in my school.	This work of art belongs in a museum.

Geodesic Structures and Tetrahedrons

Buckminster Fuller and Geodesic Domes

Geodesic domes, patented in the mid-twentieth century by Buckminster Fuller, are lightweight but sturdy hemispherical structures. Fuller considered geodesic designs a way to supply economical and energy-efficient buildings for a variety of applications. Most often, as Fuller specified, geodesic domes are constructed from prefabricated triangular segments covered with some type of thin, durable material. The triangular modules create a high strength-to-weight ratio so that the larger a geodesic dome is, the stronger it actually becomes. Without the need for interior, load-bearing walls, geodesic domes provide functional and cost-efficient use of space. The U.S. Pavilion for Expo '67 (the 1967 World's Fair and Exposition) in Montreal, Canada, was a classic example of Fuller's geodesic dome design.

Activities

▸ Construct simple tetrahedrons or more complex structures using white or colored paper. In this activity, copy paper is rolled around a pencil and glued to create a strut; many struts are used to build a structure. Toothpicks and dried peas can also be used to construct tetrahedrons. Make individual tetrahedrons or combine with others to build larger constructions.

▸ Use a two-dimensional pattern for a tetrahedron or a cube to trace, cut out, and embellish with drawings or paintings before assembling it into a three-dimensional form. Build a structure using

the forms made by the class. Discuss the differences between two-dimensional shapes and three-dimensional forms and compare the art and math terms for these concepts. Two-dimensional shapes (in art) are called plane figures in math and three-dimensional forms (in art) are called space or solid figures. (Diagrams are provided on pages 68-69)

▸ In a journal, detail the steps of the process of making a tetrahedron through writing, drawing, or a combination of both.

▸ Work collaboratively to construct elaborate, complex structures (buildings, bridges, towers, or nonobjective designs) based on the tetrahedron. Create variations by changing scale and proportion to make smaller tetrahedron units, making designs on individual struts, using different kinds of papers, and adding other materials to create mixed-media works.

▸ Use a two-dimensional pattern for a tetrahedron or a cube to trace, cut out, and embellish with intricate drawings or paintings before assembling it into a three-dimensional form. Assemble a structure using the forms made by the class.

▸ Use computer draw and/or paint software programs to create two-dimensional representations of three-dimensional tetrahedrons and other forms.

▸ In a journal, describe the steps taken by your group to make decisions, solve problems, and work together in an effective collaboration. Also describe the completed project and discuss whether or not you believe your efforts were successful.

Suggested Artworks and Artists

▸ Buckminster Fuller

Resources

Baldwin, J. *Bucky Works: Buckminster Fuller's Ideas for Today*. John Wiley and Sons, 1997.

Gurkewitz, Rona, and Bennett Arnstein. *3-D Geometric Origami: Modular Polyhedra*. Dover Publications, 1996.

The World of Buckminster Fuller, Mystic Sky video, Fox Lorber Associates, 419 Park Avenue South, New York, NY 10016.

Geodesic Structures and Tetrahedrons

Materials and Preparation

Cut a stack of 8¹/₂ x 11-in. white or colored copy paper in half to form sheets 5¹/₂ x 8 ¹/₂-in. (cut more paper as needed after students start working). Recycled paper can also be used—any type on it will not be visible on the completed structure. Assemble white glue, pencils, scissors, a skein of strong yarn for each table (yarn works best because of its elasticity), and 6-in. plastic weaving needles, one for each student. Either weaving needles or similar tools are needed to pull the yarn through the struts. If weaving needles are not available, make a wire tool by cutting wire coat hangers into approximately 6-in. lengths with a wire cutter tool. Use needle-nose pliers to bend a small hook on each end.

Technique for making individual paper rolls or "struts"

To make a standard strut, roll a piece of the 5¹/₂ x 8¹/₂-in. precut paper from the short end tightly around a pencil and glue the edge down. Roll a number of struts before beginning assembly.

Instructions for connecting struts

Start by connecting 3 struts to form a triangle. Cut a piece of yarn about 36-in. long. Pull it with the weaving needle or wire tool through 3 struts and tie them together with a double knot as tightly as possible to make a triangle. Add two more struts to the remaining yarn (if the yarn is not long enough, tie on more yarn) and tie them to the apex of the first triangle, forming a second triangle. Add one strut to one of the unconnected apexes and tie to the free apex, forming a tetrahedron. All following struts are added in this 2-then-1 pattern, each triangle sharing a side of a previous triangle.

Photo by Nancy Walkup.

Creating the structures

Assign students to collaborative working groups of 3-4 students. Each group will work together to determine the kind of geodesic structure (tower, bridge, building, etc.) they will make and the size and form it will take. Have each group make a large number of "struts" before they begin assembling their structure. Completed structures may be simple or complex, symmetrical or asymmetrical, but should be composed of equilateral triangles.

Origami

Geometric Shapes and Forms

Symmetry

Proportion

Op Art and Optical Illusions

Tessellations and other Congruent Shapes

Perspective

Graphing Responses to Works of Art

Geodesic Structures and Tetrahedrons

Origami

Origami

Origami, the art of paper folding, is traditionally associated with Japanese culture. It originated, however, in first century AD China with the invention of paper. The forerunner of modern day origami served practical purposes for the Chinese, who made useful commodities such as vases, bowls, and boxes from folded paper. Almost 500 years after paper was invented, Buddhist monks brought the secret to Japan.

The Japanese quickly integrated paper into everyday life, first using it in architecture and for ceremonial functions. With foundations in such formal usage, origami slowly evolved to become what we recognize today as Japanese paper folding. Passed from generation to generation by oral tradition between mothers and daughters, designs remained simple until about 1797 when the first written instructions for paper folding designs were published. It is interesting to note that prior to 1880 Japanese paper folding was known as orikata (folding exercises), but as designs changed to become more playful and complex, the name became origami (to fold paper).

As origami entered the realm of creativity, as opposed to its original ideal of repetition of set designs, two men (Akira Yoshizawa and Sam Randlett) developed a system of lines and arrows that simplify written instructions. This system has been adopted worldwide and has opened the doors of paper folding to an unlimited audience. Generally starting with simple designs, origami books with Yoshizawa's and Randlett's method systematically lead paperfolders from the novice stage to expert.

No matter how intricate the final design, origami adheres to the concept that the product must be achieved exclusively by folding paper (no glue, tape, staples, scissors, or other aids). Contemporary origami techniques continue to develop into seemingly impossible feats of folding. Master folders produce objects such as recognizable, anatomically correct insects with segmented bodies and multiple legs.

The practice of origami provides meaningful opportunities for students to work with geometric shapes and fractions. Please consult the resources below for more specific directions for making origami.

Suggested Artists

▶ Humiaki Huzita

▶ Robert Lang

▶ Sam Randlett

▶ Akira Yoshizawa

Resources

Brill, David. *Brilliant Origami: A Collection of Original Designs.* Japan Publications,1996.

Lang, Robert. *The Complete Book of Origami: Step-By-Step Instructions in over 1000 Diagrams/37 Original Models.* Dover, 1989.

Pearl, Barbara. *Math in Motion: Origami in the Classroom K-12.* Crane Publishing, 1994.

Coerr, Eleanor. *Sadako and the Thousand Paper Cranes.* Yearling Books, 1979.

Mitchell, David. *Mathematical Origami: Geometrical Shapes by Paper Folding.* Tarquin Publications, 1997.

Say, Allen. *Tree of Cranes.* Boston: Houghton Mifflin Co., 1991.

Kenneway, Eric. *Origami: Paperfolding for Fun.* New York: Gallery Books, 1980.

Sakata, Hideaki. *Origami.* Available from Fascinating Folds, PO Box 2820-235, Torrance, CA 90509-2820.

Diagrams

hexagon

equilateral triangle

circle

square

Diagrams

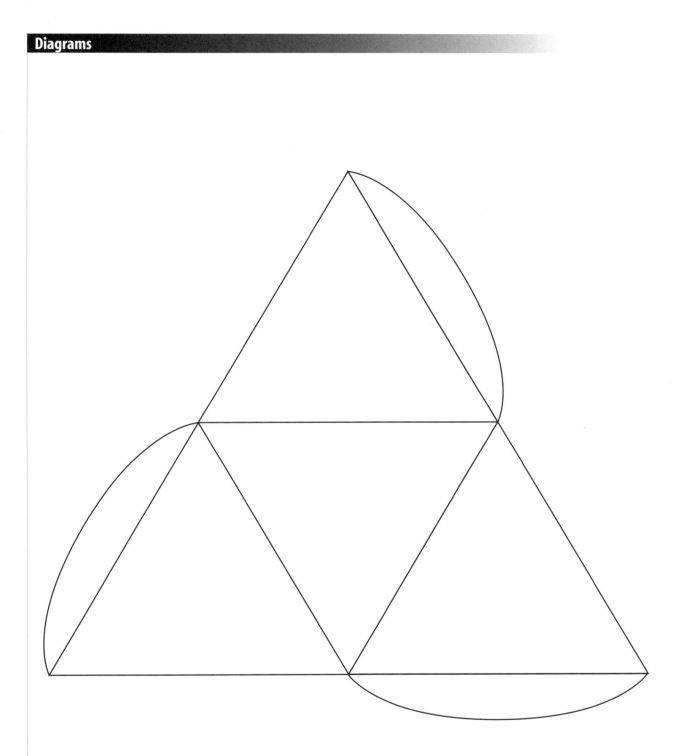

Chapter 5
Art and Performing Arts

" *Music breathing of statues. Perhaps:*

Silence of paintings. You language where all language

Ends. You time

Standing vertically on the motion of mortal hearts. "

— Rainer Marie Rilke, c. 1913-1918

Art and Performing Arts

Each area of the arts — visual, dance, music, and theatre — intricately and naturally interweaves with all the others. To ensure that these important connections are made in American classrooms, however, one overarching standard called the "Art Connections Standard" was written. The art connections standard specifies that students in every area of the arts will "understand and make connections among the various art forms and other disciplines."

This connection mandate should not be construed to mean that the arts be used to teach other subjects or that the arts be the handmaiden of other disciplines. The standard addresses and promotes two important points. These points are:

1. That learning in the arts is a valid and worthwhile academic pursuit within itself.

2. That learning through the arts places visual arts, dance, music, and theatre as central to the general curriculum.

In addition, the content standards require that students demonstrate understanding and competence in the arts, not that they master a field. That is to say that it is not expected that every student will become a professional artist, dancer, musician, or actor; but rather, that students will be furnished the tools to understand the structural systems of the arts.

Correlation

Correlation shows similarities and differences between content areas. For this reason, vocabulary is an obvious choice for correlation between the visual arts and the performing arts. Frequently, the same words can be used in one or more of the arts and mean the same or about the same thing; however, at other times the same words can have very different meanings for each subject. For example, the word "rhythm" relates to a similar concept in both art and music, whereas the word "color" represents a different concept for each area.

Recognizing and understanding the similarities and differences in vocabulary usage in the visual and performing arts is crucial in demonstrating competence in any of the various art fields. Providing opportunities for students to use

Art and Performing Arts

appropriate and correct arts vocabulary assists with development of written and spoken communication skills.

Integration

Integration is more complex than correlation. Integration is multilayered and demonstrates how two or more disciplines are mutually reinforcing. An example of integration of art and theatre can be seen in activities such as documenting how social attitudes are mirrored in the visual arts and dramatic productions from a particular time. This type of meaningful integration helps students see learning as related and whole, rather than as isolated pockets of disconnected subject matter.

Critical Analysis (Elements and Principles)

The visual arts and the performing arts all hinge upon essential structures; that is, elements and principles. The visual arts as well as the performing arts rely upon fundamental elements and principles to direct production, analysis, and discussion of works of artwork. Learning the basic vocabulary of the various art forms provides a correlated link to understanding the significant similarities and differences among the arts.

Application of Media (Production and Performance)

Communication of ideas is key to the arts. Although not constrained by tightly defined parameters, visual artists typically produce two- and three-dimensional art objects; dancers create and communicate meaning through movement; musicians and singers speak to an audience with instruments and voice; and actors tell stories with words, facial expression, and body movement. Because the arts do not strictly enforce these parameters, often the parameters overlap. It is not unusual in today's art world to hear messages that accompany visual images or for an artist's own body or body movements to be the work of art. Music can derive from street sounds and song can be poetry or readings. Embracing these overlaps of content further integrates the arts.

Cultural Awareness (Time and Place)

The content standards for the arts direct that students understand art, dance, music, and theatre in the context of culture and time. Arts history provides the cultural and historical context in which all artistic achievement is considered. Through arts history, knowledge is acquired about the contributions artists from the various fields have made to cultures and societies over time. Like all disciplines, arts history has evolved, developing theories and methods to guide inquiry and analysis. It is no longer sufficient to provide "art in the dark" slide shows and "sit and get" lectures. Students should be engaged through inquiry, discussion, collaboration, and reflection.

Questioning the Nature of the Arts (Philosophy or Aesthetics)

Communicating meaning, applying appropriate criteria to performances, and understanding characteristics and merits of an artwork are content standards from the arts that suggest students be provided opportunities to determine what is or is not properly labeled "art." When big questions about the arts such as "Is it art?" or "What is art?" are posed, students are given occasions to express reasoned opinions substantiated by facts that have been drawn from critical analysis, production experiences, and history.

Bridging the Arts

The National Content Standards provide a framework from which teachers can build meaningful activities and units of studies that allow students to think about the arts, talk about the arts, write about the arts, and create in the arts. This chapter presents activities for integrating art with dance, music, and theatre.

Resources

Barrett, T. *Talking about Student Art*. Davis Publications: Worchester, MA, 1997.

Dixon, N., Davies, and Politano, C. *Building Connections: Learning with Readers Theatre*. Peguis Publishers Ltd., Winnipeg, Canada, 1996.

http://www.storyarts.org/
Curriculum ideas exchange, articles, and links for using storytelling in the classroom

Students reenact *Tar Beach* by Faith Ringgold. Photo by Nancy Walkup.

Fine Arts Theatre

Fine Arts Theatre

Living Paintings

Sequencing

Three-Way Contrast and Comparison

Be a Critic

Three-Dimensional Band

Multilayered Painting

Sounds from Around the World

Aural Pictures

Students reenact *Tar Beach* by Faith Ringgold. Photo by Nancy Walkup.

Fine Arts Theatre

Reader's Theatre is a process that invites students to engage in writing of scripts, reading aloud, and performing with a purpose. Fine Arts Theatre, somewhat similar to Reader's Theatre, is comprised of a variety of components also related to communication:

▶ Art observation,

▶ Writing, composing, or choreographing individual or group parts, and

▶ Reading aloud, singing, dancing, or playing musical instruments individually or with groups.

Fine Arts Theatre can be as small as a classroom presentation or as a large as a school-wide assembly. Fine Arts Theatre can encompass any number of the arts. Stressing predominantly oral communication about a work of art through a variety of art forms, Fine Arts Theatre is not traditional theatre.

Directions

▶ For small productions, place students in collaborative groups with at least six members. For larger productions such as school-wide assemblies, an entire class may wish to create and present their own Fine Arts Theatre production.

▶ Provide each group with a reproduction of a work of art to interpret through music, a play, poetry, dance, singing, or any combination of the fine arts.

▶ Distribute the Fine Arts Theatre notes handout to each group.

▶ Ask students to brainstorm and then write words, phrases, and sentences about their work of art.

▶ Using the brainstormed words, phrases, and sentences, ask students to write a summative sentence about what they think is the meaning of the work of art.

▶ If available, give students printed information about the artwork and artist; otherwise, ask students to research the art object and maker. Is the students' interpretation of the artwork similar to the artist's intent?

▶ Ask students to contemplate how they can best communicate to an audience about the artwork and its meaning. Options might include sound, movement, reading, singing, a play, or any combination of the fine arts.

▶ If desired, poetry or prose formats from the Art and Language Arts chapter in *Bridging the Curriculum through Art* may be used; however, any poetry or prose format is applicable to Fine Arts Theatre.

▶ When students have completed their interpretation of the work of art, allow time for rehearsal and final editing.

▶ Display the art reproduction where it is visible to the entire audience. Present the Fine Arts Theatre to small or large groups.

Suggested Works of Art

▶ Any artwork that tells a story.

Fine Arts Theatre Note Page

Living Paintings

Students reenact *Detroit Industry* by Diego Rivera. Photo by Nancy Walkup.

Living Paintings

As the title suggests, Living Paintings involve the use of a painting (or other work of art) presented in such a way as to personify the characters within the image. Predominate to the presentation is the backdrop, costumes, motion, music, and script. Presentations may be art historical (about the time and place of the work or the artist), involve criticism (description, analysis, and interpretation), include aesthetic debates (Is it art?), or tell how the work was created (production).

The backdrop for a Living Painting is pivotal to the success of the activity because the backdrop provides the setting for the entire presentation. The backdrop should be a large student-rendered reproduction of a masterwork. Students act the parts of characters within the image; therefore all characters (animals, people, or main objects) are not included in the backdrop.

One easy and economical way to create a large backdrop is to tape together long strips of white craft paper. A good size for a Living Painting backdrop is about 6-ft. x 8-ft. An opaque projector can be used to project the image on the paper for duplication. Students can then paint with tempera or use paper cutouts to re-create the masterwork. If desired, a large wooden frame can be built to support the backdrop. More than one backdrop can be held on a single frame if only the top edge is connected to the frame (like a flip chart). Backdrops can be stored on the frame and used more than once.

Directions

▶ Assign various jobs to the entire class. Jobs will include:

Backdrop painters

Stagehands

Researchers

Scriptwriters

Actors and narrators

Other jobs may also be necessary. In most instances, every student will work on the backdrop in addition to one or more other jobs.

▶ Select an art object for students to research, write about, and present as a class production.

▶ Effective presentations include students presenting information from the point-of-view of the artist or characters within the image.

▶ Students not participating as narrators should be included as other characters.

▶ The most interesting Living Paintings go beyond tableaus and include movement and music. When selecting music, keep in mind the meaning of the work of art as well as the meaning of the music. For example, although it is a temptation to include a tune such as Rossini's *William Tell Overture* when depicting scenes from the work of Charles Russell, a meaningful integration of art and music would include music that was created during the time of the artwork or music that is about horses, cowboys, or the American West.

Suggested Works of Art

Artworks that are narrative and include a variety of characters

Living Paintings

Students reenact *Detroit Industry* by Diego Rivera. Photo by Nancy Walkup.

Sequencing

Photo by Nancy Walkup

Sequencing

Sequencing offers students the chance to infer what came before or led up to an event, show what is happening in the present, and predict what is likely to happen next. Based upon clues found within a work of art, inference and prediction can be readily explored.

Directions

As an extension to the Living Painting, the same backdrops can be utilized for three different presentations: before, now, and later.

▸ Assign students to teams of two or three.

▸ Provide the sequencing handout for each group and display an art reproduction where every student can readily view it.

▸ Use the sequencing handout as a planning page for an extension to the Living Painting.

▸ Encourage students to use clues within the artwork to make appropriate inferences about what happened first and predictions about what will happen next. Guesses or flights of the imagination not supported by evidence within the works of art should be avoided.

▸ Set a time frame for the sequence such as "just a moment ago, now, and in five minutes" or "a year ago, the present, a year later."

▸ The sequence can be about a time span related to the characters and action in the image or can be about the processes used by the artist to create the work of art (for example, planning, creating, and exhibition.)

▸ Use the planning page to sketch characters, create costumes, show movements, and suggest types of music that show change over time.

Variation

▸ Provide each student with an art postcard and sequencing worksheet. Ask students to sketch before and after scenes and then to write a paragraph about each. Be certain that sketches and paragraphs are supported by clues found within the masterwork.

Suggested Works of Art

▸ Narrative works that include characters and suggest a sense of time and place

Sequencing: Before, Now, and After

▶ Look carefully at an art image. What clues in the artwork help you to decide what happened before? What clues in the art image help you to predict what will happen next?

▶ In the top frame, draw what you think happened before.

▶ In the bottom frame, draw what you predict will happen next.

Three-Way Contrast and Comparison

Fine Arts Theatre

Living Paintings

Sequencing

Three-Way Contrast and Comparison

Be a Critic

Three-Dimensional Band

Multilayered Painting

Sounds from Around the World

Aural Pictures

Photo by Nancy Walkup.

Three-Way Contrast and Comparison

Contrasting and comparing works of art helps students to isolate unique characteristics of works of art, art styles, art techniques, or any number of other topics. Learning to classify characteristics and then examine them for similarities and differences helps to frame the visual arts and performing arts within the context of time and culture. Somewhat similar to the Venn Diagram, this three-way contrast and comparison is more complex and leads the way to further discussion, writing, and the use of timelines.

Directions

▶ Students may work independently or in pairs.

▶ Distribute a Three-Way Contrast and Comparison worksheet to each student or team.

▶ After a class discussion about the characteristics of any art style, ask students to write the unique characteristics of the art style in the first column.

▶ Provide students with an assortment of art reproductions. To make this assignment challenging, one art reproduction should be from the style discussed, one art reproduction should have some of the characteristics of the style discussed, and one art reproduction should not have any of the characteristics discussed.

▶ Ask students to select the image that best represents the style discussed, write the title and artist's name in the second column, and list five or more clues that support the classification.

▶ For the final column, ask students to select another art form (that is, dance, music, or theatre).

▶ After a dance, piece of music, or dramatic production is selected, ask students to list five or more characteristics that helped them to place the performance within the context of the art style.

▶ Using the worksheet, ask students to write a research paper that includes:

    ▶ A complete description of the art style.

    ▶ A complete description of the work of art and why it is classified as the style.

    ▶ A complete description of the performance and why it is classified as the style.

    ▶ A paragraph that explains what the style, artwork, and performance have in common and what is different about them.

▶ Ask students to share their research with the class.

▶ Display the worksheets and research papers with the works of art they discuss.

Suggested Works of Art

▶ Works that readily fit the style of art studied

▶ Works that obviously do not fit the style of art studied

▶ Works that have some characteristics of the style studied

Three-Way Contrast and Comparison Chart

Art style	Title of artwork	Title of artwork
Approximate dates of the style	Name of artist	Name of artist
	Date of artwork	Date of artwork
	Country or culture of origin	Country or culture of origin
List five or more important characteristics of this art style.	List five or more clues found in this work of art that help you decide the art style.	List five or more clues found in this performance that help you to decide the style.
1.	1.	1.
2.	2.	2.
3.	3.	3.
4.	4.	4.
5.	5.	5.

After you have filled in all three columns, use a blue pen to underline on your list the unique characteristics that the art style, the work of art, and the performance share with each other. Use a red pen to underline the characteristics that are unique to each artwork.

Use your notes to write a research paper that includes:

▶ A complete description of the art style.
▶ A complete description of the work of art and why it is classified as the style.
▶ A complete description of the performance and why it is classified as the style.
▶ A paragraph that explains what the style, artwork, and performance have in common and what is different about them.

Be a Critic

Edgar Degas, Café-Concert at Les Ambassadeurs, c. 1876-77, pastel over monotype on paper, Musée des Beaux-Arts, Lyons, France.

Be a Critic

▸ Students may work independently or in pairs.

▸ Ask students to locate a review in a newspaper or magazine about an art exhibition, a musical performance, or a play.

▸ How does the review describe the event?

▸ Ask students to cite examples of descriptive text within the article.

▸ How does the review encourage or discourage visits to the exhibition or performance?

▸ Again, ask students to cite examples from the text.

▸ What parts of the review are based on fact?

▸ What part on opinion?

▸ Distribute reproductions of works of art that show a musical or theatrical performance. Ask students to write a review of the performance as if they had heard the music or listened to the play.

▸ Make sure that the article includes both facts and opinions.

▸ Read the reviews aloud and then display with the artwork.

Suggested works of art

▸ Images that depict a musical or theatrical event

Critical Review

Title of the work of art _____

Look closely at the work of art. Pretend that you are visiting the event. Write as many words or phrases as you can that describe what you observe. Include facts and opinions.

Circle all of the words and phrases that are facts.

Underline all the words and phrases that are opinions.

Review your circled facts. Write one paragraph that uses only facts to describe the scene.

Review your underlined opinions. Write one paragraph that is mainly based on opinion.

Write closing remarks that will either encourage or discourage someone else to attend the event.

Three-Dimensional Band

Fine Arts Theatre

Living Paintings

Sequencing

Three-Way Contrast and Comparison

Be a Critic

Three-Dimensional Band

Multilayered Painting

Sounds from Around the World

Aural Pictures

Edgar Degas, *Orchestra of the Opera*, c. 1870. Oil on canvas, 22¹/₄ x 18¹/₄-in., Musée d'Orsay, Paris.

Three-Dimensional Band

▶ Locate images of musical bands or orchestras for students to observe and discuss.

▶ Find details within the images that visually suggest or describe the type of musical group, the time, the place, and the reason for the music.

▶ Place students in collaborative groups of six to eight.

▶ At random, assign each group a type of band such as jazz, folk, or postmodern.

▶ What types of instruments would each group require?

▶ What types of costumes would the band members wear?

▶ What posture would each band member have?

▶ How would each of these elements help to visualize how the band would sound?

▶ Provide each student with a baseball-size amount of clay to create an individual band member.

▶ Divide the clay into portions that will allow for the construction of a figure, a musical instrument, and any details that are needed.

▶ Roll a small amount of clay for a head, a larger amount for a body, and elongated portions for limbs.

▶ Demonstrate appropriate techniques for attaching clay pieces by dampening the clay parts and roughening areas to be attached.

▶ Smooth pieces together.

▶ Pose the characters to demonstrate movement (for example, bent knees, tilted head, or tapping foot).

▶ Add details with leftover clay or by carving into the clay before it dries.

▶ Allow to dry.

▶ If using clay that must be fired, bisque fire then paint or glaze.

▶ What sound does the band suggest? How does the band visually suggest this sound? How does the band suggest a certain time or place?

Variation

▶ Instruct students to research a theatrical production or dance and create a stage setting with appropriate characters.

Suggested Works of Art

▶ Works that depict musicians

Multilayered Painting

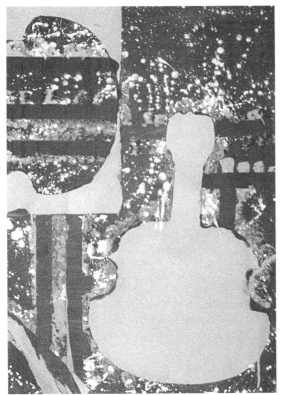

Student work, Midway Park Elementary. Photo by Pam Stephens.

Multilayered Painting

▶ Provide art reproductions that depict the performing arts.

▶ Ask students to identify symbols that represent each performer (for example, a swallow tail tuxedo coat for a symphony orchestra conductor).

▶ Students should work independently for the remainder of this lesson.

▶ Tape a 24 x 36-in. piece of drawing paper onto a sheet of heavy cardboard or other sturdy material. Using a large paintbrush, create an abstract design of broad strokes or splatters on the drawing paper.

▶ While this painting is drying, ask each student to select one of the performing arts and then to determine symbols which represent those arts.

▶ Provide poster board or other sturdy material cut into three different sizes of rectangles no smaller than 4 x 6-in. These are to be used as templates.

▶ On each template draw the outline shape of a chosen symbol. Allow the outline to touch at least three edges of the template.

▶ Cut out the shape.

▶ Place tape on the backside of the templates to hold them in place.

▶ Place the templates in a pleasing arrangement on the splatter painting.

▶ Using different colors, again paint in broad strokes or splatters or use a sponge to create a different pattern or texture. Paint over the templates.

▶ Allow to dry. Do not remove the templates.

▶ Lightly apply 3–5 strips of tape across the surface of the painting to create a unifying pattern across the picture plane.

▶ Using different colors, paint with different strokes, splatter, or sponge so that the paint covers the templates and tape.

▶ Allow to dry. Remove the tape and templates.

▶ How do the symbols represent one or more of the performing arts?

Suggested Works of Art

▶ Works that depict music, dance, or theatre

Sounds from Around the World

Fine Arts Theatre

Living Paintings

Sequencing

Three-Way Contrast and Compare

Be a Critic

Three-Dimensional Band

Multilayered Painting

Sounds from Around the World

Aural Pictures

Sounds from Around the World

Music has played an important role in all cultures throughout time. As a result, many instruments have been created to produce sounds that are indigenous to particular times and places.

▶ Ask students to research the musical instruments listed here or identify others to research.

▶ Locate on a world map where the instruments are or have been commonly used.

▶ Ask students to report to the class about the country or culture of origin, the design of the instrument, the use of the instrument for producing music, and the sound the instrument produces.

Suggested Instruments to Research

Aulos	Ancient Greek double reed instrument that had two pipes
Balalaika	Triangular-shaped Russian string instrument similar to a guitar
Buisine	Medieval straight trumpet
Dulcitar	A modern instrument that combines the dulcimer with a guitar
Lute	A half-pear shaped stringed instrument of Arabian origins
Ocarina	Small flute usually made from clay
Samisen	Japanese lute
Saron	A Northern Indian percussion instrument similar to a xylophone
Zither	String folk instrument from the Austrian and Bavarian Alps

Variations for Research Topics

▶ Similar to musical performances, dance and drama reflect the ideas and beliefs of cultures throughout time. Also similar to the visual arts, music, dance, and drama have not always been created with the intent of being art. For what other reasons might people create objects, music, dance, or drama?

▶ Explore dances or dramatic presentations from around the world. Ask students to identify dances or dramatic presentations from a variety of cultures and times. What do these dances and dramatic presentations tell us about place and time?

▶ How do dancers and actors communicate ideas? Contrast and compare communication through the visual arts to communication through dance or drama.

Aural Pictures

Fine Arts Theatre

Living Paintings

Sequencing

Three-Way Contrast and Comparison

Be a Critic

Three-Dimensional Band

Multilayered Painting

Sounds from Around the World

Aural Pictures

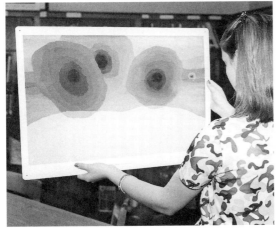

Foghorns, Arthur Dove. Photo by Nancy Walkup.

Aural Pictures

▸ Students should work independently.

▸ Listen to a variety of musical pieces that have diverse instrumental sounds such as those produced by cymbals or harp strings.

▸ Ask students to describe how the various instruments sound.

▸ Now ask students to think about how they would visually describe those sounds. For example, clashing cymbals might be visually described as very jagged and vividly colored while sounds of a harp might be rounded and in muted colors.

▸ Look at art reproductions that suggest sound such as Arthur Dove's *Foghorns*. How have artists visually suggested the idea of sound?

▸ Ask students to decide upon an instrument whose sound they would like to visually create.

▸ Distribute sheets of 9 x 12-in. construction or drawing paper.

▸ Ask students to draw a line or shape that represents the sound of the instrument they have selected.

▸ Begin the line on one edge of the paper and extend it to another edge.

▸ Repeat the line across the picture plane until the picture plane is filled.

▸ Use two or more colors of paint, markers, or other media to complete the aural picture. On another sheet of paper, draw the instrument that has produced the sound. Cut out this instrument and glue it to the aural picture.

▸ How does the visual representation symbolize the sound of the selected musical instrument?

Suggested Works of Art

▸ *Foghorns* by Arthur Dove

▸ Any work that suggests sound

Chapter 6
Art and Science

"*Scientists and artists both require a keen sense of observation, vital powers of imagination, the persistence to achieve their visions through hard work and perseverance in the face of many challenges, and the ability to communicate their discoveries to a broader audience.*"

— Diane Shaw, Co-curator,
Science and the Artist's Book, the Smithsonian

Art and Science

Scientific themes, especially those related to the natural environment, frequently are reflected in works of art. Artists throughout time and from many different cultures have reproduced scenes from their surroundings, documenting the world as the artist sees it. These scenes from the natural world, usually classified as landscapes, invite us to explore the sometimes realistic and sometimes fantastic depictions of the artist's interpretations. Many times these artworks of the natural world raise more questions than they answer, perhaps causing us to examine our use of the earth's resources, demanding that we think about the future of the environment, or simply giving us pause to contemplate the power and beauty of nature. Think of the meticulously accurate historic paintings of birds by American John James Audubon or *Great Wave Off Kanagawa*, the majestic and fearfully powerful image of a tsunami, an engulfing wave of the sea, by the Japanese master Hokusai.

Beyond the natural environment, however, works of art and the processes and tools used by artists connect with other science concepts. Through meaningful art exploration, many learning objectives set forth by both the National Standards for the Visual Arts and the National Standards for Science are met. Requirements for creating enduring works of art include that artists understand concepts similar to those practiced by scientists. These related concepts encompass theories, facts, rules, and guidelines as a foundation for the design and creation of art objects.

Photo by Nancy Walkup.

Inquiry, Problem-Solving, and Evaluation

Both art and science require that students develop skills such as careful observation, reasoning, and prediction in order to draw conclusions and justify interpretations. Further, both content areas mandate that students become proficient in posing questions, designing problems based upon those questions, then finding and evaluating solutions based upon collected data. Art and science also share a hands-on discovery approach.

Science Domains

Art production, art discussion, and art writing activities can provide concrete examples for exploration of science topics such as mass, matter, and chemical reactions. For example, what does a sculptor need to know about mass and matter? Why do printmakers need to understand how certain chemicals react with each other? Why do painters need to know if the colors they use will remain true over time? When students participate in activities that allow them to think and act as artists facing these problems, meaningful solutions result because the scientific concept has been applied to a real-life experience.

Technology

In art and science, students are furnished opportunities to develop competency in decision-making. Technology in both content areas emphasizes that students develop fundamental abilities associated with the process of design or planning. For example, in art as well as in science, students identify and state problems, plan and implement solutions, and then evaluate the effectiveness of the solution. Students who are able to isolate a design problem, state it, and then think through to a logical solution are applying critical thinking skills that relate to everyday situations.

Technology also holds two fundamental applications for the correlation of art and science, as it may be addressed through graphic, structural, and organizational design or through the use of media. The computer can be used for the presentation of content or as a medium for creating art. The rapid growth of the Internet and related technologies has already created a demand for the expertise of people knowledgeable about both art and science.

Personal and Social Perspectives

Through observation and interpretation of masterworks or by creating works of art that depict local, national, or global environments, students are better able to visualize the impact of society upon the natural world. Contemplating personal and social issues through works of art help students to understand better the characteristics of populations, resources, and the environment and the impact that individuals and groups have upon them.

Chrysler Concorde LXi interior. Courtesy Chrysler Motor Company.

History

Science, like art, has its own history. It is a history that continues and is rapidly changing. By studying the chronologies of art and science, students are able to see the role that both fields have played in the development of cultures throughout time. By studying the histories of art and science, students can track the change in approaches to artistic and scientific inquiry and production. Additionally, the impact that science has had upon art and the ways that art has depicted science can be readily perceived. For example, tracking the history of art materials and media over time would be a meaningful exercise to discover how scientific developments have impacted the art world. Many of today's students may be surprised to discover that paints were not always available in premixed, ready-to-use tubes and that artists in the past had to grind and mix their own.

Art, Science, and Writing

Artists and scientists write in diaries or journals about their daily work. Likewise, students can write in diaries or journals about their art and science activities. Artists and scientists write notations about their work, describe problems, and brainstorm solutions in sketchbooks or notebooks. Similarly, students can sketch and write about their work, problems, and solutions to problems.

Artists and scientists write sequential steps to follow in the creation of artworks or formulas. Students can write the steps they take to create an artwork or to devise an experiment. The sketchbooks of artist and inventor Leonardo da Vinci, the original Renaissance man and interdisciplinary model, provide a fine subject of study for this approach. In his sketchbooks, da Vinci recorded drawings of his artwork and inventions along with written notes and ideas.

Writing summary sentences, elaborating upon details, finding main ideas, predicting outcomes, pinpointing causes and effects — the list of writing topics for art and science is virtually endless. Whether working individually or in groups of two or more, writing about art and science experiences helps students develop stronger communication skills and is a valuable component of any interdisciplinary connection.

Careers that Require both Art and Science

Students with a strong interest in art and science may want to consider careers that combine both interests. Medical and scientific illustrators, graphic artists, website and software designers, industrial and product designers, and architects all need to possess significant understandings of both art and science. Nevertheless, all students can benefit from meaningful educational experiences that are based on art and science.

The Scientific Method and Art Criticism

The Scientific Method and Art Criticism

Isaac Newton first proposed the scientific method, an approach to scientific study, in 1687. It is a standard approach to conducting scientific experiments that involves asking a question based on observation and stating a testable hypothesis or plausible answer. The next steps include constructing or designing a study to answer the hypothesis, gathering data, interpreting the results, and drawing conclusions using critical and analytical thinking skills. Consider the theoretical approach to art criticism that includes description, analysis, interpretation, and judgment. Can you explain the similarities between the two approaches? Do the steps of art criticism need to be sequential or can they occur in any order? Choose a work of art to investigate and have students complete the worksheet on the following page in the order of their preference.

Courtesy Dallas Museum of Art. Photo by Nancy Walkup

The Scientific Method and Art Criticism

Name of Artwork: _____

Name of Artist: _____

Date of Artwork: _____

Description: _____

_____

_____

_____

Analysis: _____

_____

_____

_____

Interpretation: _____

_____

_____

_____

Judgment: _____

_____

_____

_____

Reflections on Making Comparisons between Art Criticism and the Scientific Method:
(complete on the back of the page)

Color Theory

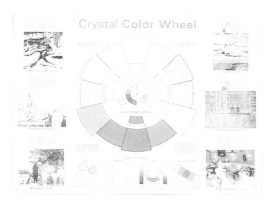

The Color Wheel

The first color wheel was designed by the scientist Isaac Newton. The color wheel familiar to artists depicts the primary (red, blue, and yellow) and secondary colors (green, orange, and violet), but it applies only to pigments such as paint. The color wheel used in photography and the science of optics is not the same, as it is based on the characteristics of the wavelengths of light–electromagnetic radiation–either natural or artificial. The difference results from the fact that pigment and light are perceived differently by the human eye. For instance, a combination of red and green paint is perceived as brown, but a combination of red and green light is viewed as yellow. Our eyes can only distinguish a small section of the electromagnetic spectrum–the visible light. Different colors across the spectrum correspond to different wavelengths and allow us to see in color.

Color Theory for Light

In optics, the primary colors are red, blue, and green, and the secondary, or complementary, colors are yellow, cyan, and magenta. White light contains the entire spectrum of colors—all wavelengths of visible light. Color mixing in optics is either additive or subtractive. When beams of light are mixed, the viewer sees only the wavelengths that are selectively given off. To see how a prism separates light into a spectrum, the wavelengths of visible light shine a light through a prism. The colors that appear are the same as in a rainbow, in which raindrops act as prisms.

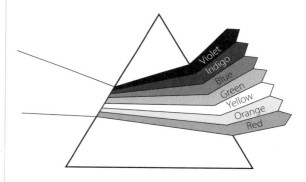

Color Theory for Pigment and Paint

Using watercolor or gouache (opaque watercolor) paints, complete the color wheel on the following page with appropriate colors of paint.

Resources

Birren, Faber. *Principles of Color: A Review of Past Traditions and Modern Theories of Color Harmony.* Schiffer Publishing, 1987.

Wilcox, Michael. *Blue and Yellow Don't Make Green.* North Light Books, 1994.

Color Wheel for Pigment and Paint

Using watercolor or gouache (opaque watercolor) paints, complete the color wheel with appropriate colors of paint, mixing only red, blue, and yellow paints.

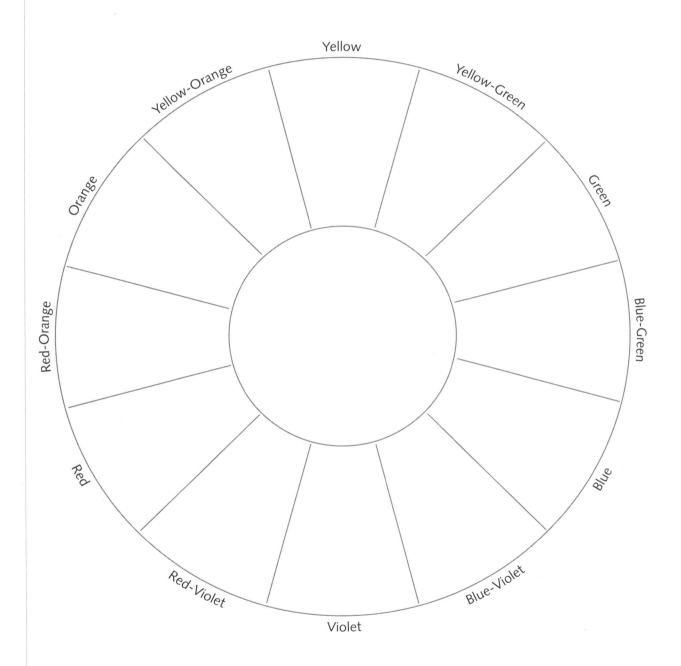

Timeline of Art Materials

Timeline of Art Materials

Why do painters need to know if the colors they use will remain true over time? Why do printmakers need to understand how certain chemicals interact with each other? How did the invention of acrylic paint change painting? Which chemicals make up the ingredients for a ceramic glaze? Technological advances in media continue to prompt changes in the materials and methods that artists use. Compare this timeline of art materials with historical events of the same time periods.

Timeline of Art Materials

By Sharon Warwick

20,000 BC	Cave dwellers paint on stone walls with pigments as civilization develops. Paints are made from charcoal, manganese ore, clay and lime, animal blood, and iron compounds. Earliest ceramics may have been used in social activities or religious rituals that involved the making and firing of goddess and animal figures.
9500 BC	Fired vessels created in Japan.
4000 BC	Potters in the Middle East develop the pottery wheel.
3000 BC	Egyptians paint on paper-like material from papyrus plant fibers and use watercolors to decorate tomb walls and ornamental objects.
2700 BC	Egyptians create the first ceramic glaze.
400 BC	Encaustic, melted beeswax and pigment, painting used widely in Greece and Rome. By 800 AD, encaustic painting is abandoned, but followed by two encaustic revivals in 1754 and from the 1940s to the present.
AD 100	Chinese artists use paper made from bark from mulberry and bamboo trees.
300-980	Clay artists in Teotihuacan, Mexico, produce a variety of pottery using fresco, an unfired technique, to decorate ritual vessels.
800	European artists begin to use paper made from cotton or linen rags.
1100s	Ultramarine blue, ground lapis lazuli, used as a pigment by the Assyrians and Babylonians.
1200s	Paper made from linen fiber comes into use.
1300-1500s	Egg tempera used on wooden panels primarily in Italy.
1400s	Egg tempera is highly developed in Flanders, the process for purification of linseed oil is published, and products for distillation of alcohol become commercially available.
1500	Delftware produced in Delft, Holland. Special blue and white tin-glazed pottery in which the Dutch added a second firing to the Italian single firing technique.
1500s	Egg tempera becomes obsolete, but is revived later and used into the 20th century.
1600-1700s	Oil paints universally used for easel painting.
1600-1750	English slipware made in which fine, liquid clay is used to trail a pattern on earthenware.
1700s	Oil pastels begin to be used for portraiture, zinc white first made and sold in France, and watercolor techniques are developed in England, France, and the Netherlands.
1724	Prussian blue introduced in England.
1750-1800s	Rose madder used.
1797	Chrome colors first used in red, orange, and yellow.
1700-1800s	Artists become increasingly dependent on commonly manufactured art materials.
1800s	Lead pencil in wooden case comes into use; zinc white introduced to American artists although it is not widely used until the 1900s.
1820s	Cobalt blue introduced in France.
1828-1830	Cadmium replaces chrome in yellows because of its more permanent qualities.
1834	Chinese white prepared for watercolor by Winsor & Newton of England.
1870	Cerulean blue introduced in Europe.
1900	Alizarin supersedes Rose Madder as color of choice for red.
1919	Titanium white introduced in Norway and America.
1945	Synthetic binders are developed, making acrylic and vinyl paint available.

The History and Chemistry of Ceramics

Photo by Nancy Walkup

The History and Chemistry of Ceramics

From their earliest times, humans have used the properties of clay to their advantage, molding and firing mixtures of clay, sand, gypsum, or straw to form vessels sometimes decorated with paints or glazes made from plants or ground, colored pigments. Similar technologies extended to the use of adobe, a combination of mud and straw, as a building material. Even today adobe buildings shelter many people in dry, desert regions of the world.

Ancient Times

Humans have carved images into clay and created clay figurines such as goddesses and animals from about 35,000 BC, but the beginning of ceramic history is equated with the first instance of fired clay vessels. Since dried, unfired clay breaks apart easily, the discovery that clay objects are much stronger if fired at a high temperature was a technological advance. It is believed that the first clay firing occurred in Japan from 10,000 to 7000 BC. More recent discoveries in Czechoslovakia have uncovered The Goddess Dolni Vestonice, a figurine from about 25,000 BC.

At around the same time Jomon pottery appeared in Japan, countries in the Middle East began developing vessels to carry water or food items. The earliest pottery-making industry developed in the Middle East before 6500 BC. With the establishment of cities in the Middle East, people started inscribing records and lists on clay tablets around 4,000 BC.

The Egyptians introduced the first ceramic glazes in approximately 2700 BC. When applied to ceramic objects and fired at high temperatures, glazes produce a glass-like appearance on pottery. Early glazes were made from water and naturally occurring chemicals such as quartz, sand, zircon, barium carbonate, or other additives and pigments. Glazes can be either clear or opaque and applied by painting, dipping, or spraying. They also can be used to make a vessel waterproof.

From 2600 BC to approximately 1500, ceramic objects and techniques unique to specific cultures developed. The Banshan culture in China (2600 BC) created pottery jars painted with red and black pigments. Unglazed earthenware Haniwa figures, objects placed around burial mounds to protect the deceased, were made in Japan from 200-600. Between 300 and 980, Mexico produced vessels decorated with a process that involved layers of stucco or plaster on the outside of the piece. Tang potters from China (618-906) created white porcelain ware decorated with lead glazes in yellow (iron), blue (cobalt), and green (copper). In North America, Southwest Native American tribes made distinctively stylized decorated pottery from 800 to the present. The above pottery styles and techniques represent just a few of the innovations across the world during this time.

The History and Chemistry of Ceramics

Modern Times

Although many cultures created pottery for religious or ceremonial reasons, from the sixteenth to twentieth centuries, pottery was often made solely for decorative use. Soft-paste porcelain, a European substitute for popular Chinese porcelain, was used to make ornate items such as clocks from 1575-1804. The Ch'ing Dynasty in China (1644-1912) is well known for delicately decorated vases using highly refined glazes. The Arts and Crafts movements in Great Britain (1850-1910) and America (1800-1920), though referred to by the same name, had relatively different goals. In Great Britain artists disliked mass-produced art objects and worked to produce only handmade items. Americans also produced unique items, though not necessarily in response to the Industrial Revolution.

Ceramics developed in the 20th century with the Bauhaus School in Germany, which combined clay with a variety of other materials. By the mid-1900s, clay evolved from a functional or decorative medium into an art form. Pablo Picasso and other well-known painters starting creating ceramic artwork. Today, ceramics can take almost any form, often painted with abstract, naturalistic, or surreal images. Artists now have access to commercial glazes, though many artists still prefer to mix their own.

Timeline

10,000 – 7000 BC	Jomon pottery in Japan
before 6500 BC	Earliest pottery-making industry develops in the Middle East
4000 BC	Clay tablets used for records and lists
2700 BC	Egyptians introduced the first ceramic glaze
2600 BC	Banshan in China make pottery painted with red and black pigments
2600 BC – 1500	Ceramic techniques develop that are unique to specific cultures
200-600	Haniwa figures were made in Japan
618-906	Tang potters in China create white porcelain ware decorated with lead glazes
300-980	Mexico produced vessels decorated with layers of stucco or plaster
800-1400	Native American tribes make decorated pottery
1575-1804	Soft-paste porcelain used in Europe as a substitute for Chinese porcelain
1644-1912	Highly refined glaze formulas developed for porcelain in China
1850-1910	Arts and Crafts movements in1800-1920 Great Britain and America
1950s-present	Clay changes from functional or decorative medium into an art form

Activities

▶ Experiment with pinch, coil, and slab techniques.

▶ Collect local clay (with permission) and experiment with using it.

▶ Borrowing a method of ancient artists, make natural pigments from different colors of earth.

   Collect different colors of soil and dirt and clean them of any loose debris. Individually grind each color to a powder with a mortar and pestle or crush with a rolling pin or hammer. Place each color in a small jar with a little water. Experiment to determine the exact amount of water that will result in slip, a relatively smooth and liquid paste. Use the slip for painting or decorating a clay vessel.

▶ Try using the slip to make watercolor paintings.

▶ Research the "recipes" available for making contemporary glazes. Using only chemicals that pose no safety hazards, try mixing and firing some.

▶ Compare and contrast two ceramic pieces from two different cultures and time periods (historic/contemporary, Native American/Mexican, Native American/Japanese, etc.).

▶ Compare and contrast the pottery traditions of the Eight Northern Pueblos in New Mexico. Each of the Pueblos has particular and different clay traditions from the others. Pay special attention to the origin of the clay and design characteristics.

▶ Choose one of the Eight Northern Pueblos to discover how the arrival of Europeans affected their pottery, and find out how the coming of the railroad and competition for collectors and tourists influenced and changed their pottery.

▶ Assemble a number of clay objects, some made by hand, some made on a potter's wheel, and some manufactured. Compare the objects and discuss their perceived value. For example, is a piece more valuable if it is made by hand or made in a mold? Is an object more valuable if it is the only one or if there are many others just like it? Which of the pieces should be in a museum? Why?

Symmetry in Science

Symmetry in Science
Bilateral Symmetry

Bilateral or mirror symmetry is a type of balance in which the two halves of a whole are each other's mirror images. The parts on either side of a centerline reflect each other and are exactly the same (in science, art, and math) or nearly the same (as in approximate symmetry in science and art). A centerline, called the line of symmetry, divides an image or object in half so that one side mirrors the other. Bilateral symmetry is widely found in nature (think of the animal backbones) and seems to be pleasing to the human eye. For instance, it has been suggested that human faces that are the most symmetrical are considered the most beautiful.

Bilateral symmetry is a consequence of forward motion in living creatures. For example, though a lizard has left and right sides that mirror each other, its front and back ends are not the same. The front end has a head and arms; the back end supports larger legs and a tail that provide the ability to move forward. For movement forward to be efficient, the two sides must be balanced.

Cylindrical Symmetry

An axis is a straight line about which an object rotates or may be supposed to rotate. Objects that radiate around a vertical axis, such as a hot air balloon, a parachute, or a jellyfish, are examples of cylindrical symmetry. Cylindrically symmetrical objects do not have left or right sides and their tops and bottoms are different from each other. Every element is the same size and shape as it rotates around the vertical axis.

Photo by Nancy Walkup.

Radial or Spherical Symmetry

Another kind of symmetry that is similar to cylindrical symmetry is radial (two-dimensional) or spherical (three-dimensional) symmetry. As in cylindrical symmetry, there are no left or right sides, but the top and bottom are the same and all elements are evenly spaced around the axis. Radial symmetry can be found in living things (flowers, starfish, jellyfish), natural objects (crystals, snowflakes), human-made objects (kaleidoscopes, wheels, clock faces), and works of art.

Activities

▶ Make freestanding animals from construction paper by folding the paper in half and using the line of symmetry as the backbone. Cut away or add paper as desired.

▶ Display and discuss examples of radial cut paper designs from different cultures such as Eastern Europe, Pennsylvania Dutch, or Chinese, then make radial designs by folding and cutting colored paper.

▶ Use natural and human-made examples of symmetry as the subject for works of art.

▶ Orchids may be the only flowers that have bilateral symmetry. Conduct research to discover why, then use orchids for the subject of an artwork.

Resources

Hargittai, Istvan, and Hargittai, Magdolna. *Symmetry: A Unifying Concept*. Bolinas, CA: Shelter Publications, 1994.

Natural Science: Ecosystems and Biomes

Student mural, Daggett Middle School, Fort Worth, Texas. Photo by Nancy Walkup.

Natural Science: Ecosystems and Biomes

Scientific themes, especially those related to the natural environment, frequently are depicted in works of art. Images of environments, ecosystems, or biomes, usually classified as landscapes or seascapes, employ science as the subject of art and reflect the artist's fascination with the natural world. Landscapes are artworks in which natural scenery such as land, sky, trees, mountains, rivers, or lakes are the main feature. Though people may appear in landscapes, the natural setting itself is the main subject. In science terms, landscapes can be said to feature ecosystems and biomes.

According to *Ecosystems, Biomes, and Watersheds: Definitions and Use*, a Congressional Research Report made available in 1993 by The Committee for the National Institute for the Environment, an ecosystem is a "community of organisms interacting with one another and with the chemical and physical factors making up their environment." Similarly, the Habitat Restoration Group defines an ecosystem as "the dynamic and interrelating complex of plants and animal communities and their associated nonliving environment." The sun is the ultimate source of all energy in an ecosystem.

A related concept, the biome, is described by the Congressional report as a "major regional community of plants and animals with similar life forms and environmental conditions, named after the dominant type of life form, such as tropical rain forest, grassland, or coral reef." The Habitat Restoration Group defines biomes as "ecosystems where several habitats intersect." The average rainfall and temperature determine the patterns and boundary lines of the different biomes of the world. Biosphere 2, constructed in Arizona, is an example of a human-made biome.

Though these terms, often used interchangeably with the word environment, possess no universally accepted definitions or categories among scientists, these generalizations will be used herein to provide useful concepts for understanding biological systems.

Suggested Artworks and Artists

- Thomas Hart Benton
- Albert Bierstadt
- Rosa Bonheur
- Christo & Jeanne Claude
- Frederic Church
- Thomas Cole
- John Steuart Curry
- Grandma Moses
- Ando Hiroshige
- Katsushika Hokusai
- David Hockney
- Thomas Moran
- Georgia O'Keeffe
- Pictorial Navajo weavings

Natural Science: Ecosystems and Biomes

Photo by Nancy Walkup.

Terrestrial Biomes

Eight terrestrial biomes found on a global scale include:

Tundra: long cold winters, permafrost; low precipitation; treeless, with low shrubs, mosses, and lichens; found in the high latitudes of the northern hemisphere in a belt around the Arctic Ocean.

Taiga/Boreal Forest/Evergreen Coniferous Forest: subarctic; long cold winters, short cool summers; 16-24 inches of rain annually; found south of the tundra as a belt of coniferous trees across the northern hemisphere.

Temperate Deciduous Forest: four definite seasons, precipitation evenly distributed throughout the year, fertile soil, and 30-60 inches of rainfall per year; found in Japan, eastern North America, China, and Europe.

Temperate Grasslands/Prairie/Steppe: hot summers and cold winters; a cover of perennial grasses; 15-30 inches of rainfall per year; found in the interiors of land masses.

Desert: arid climate, with evaporation exceeding rainfall; temperature undergoes extreme variations every day, with hot days and cold nights; poor soil; vegetation consists of grasses, shrubs, cacti, and evergreen or deciduous shrubs; only 1-10 inches of rainfall annually.

Dry Scrubland/Chapparal: hot, dry summers, cool, moist winters; aromatic herbs and evergreen shrubs; thin, rocky soil.

Tropical Grassland/Savanna: dry and rainy seasons; cover of perennial grasses in tropical wet and dry climates; scattered trees and shrubs; often found on either side of rainforests.

Rainforest/Tropical Evergreen Forest: warm, moist tropical lowlands; high temperature and rainfall, over 60 inches rainfall per year; tall trees, layers of vegetation; found in equatorial regions.

Resources

Corn, M. Lynne. (1993). Ecosystems, Biomes, and Watersheds: Definitions and Use. Available from the Committee for the National Institute for the Environment, 1725 K Street, NW, Suite 212, Washington, D.C. 20006 (202) 530-5810.

Habitat Restoration Group, RRM Design Group, P.O. Box 4006, Felton, CA 95018, 831/335-6800.

Sample Biome Activities

- Make a folding "screen" that depicts a particular biome/ecosystem through all four seasons. To begin, accordion-fold a 9 x 24-in. piece of colored construction paper or other board into four equal parts, creating a folding screen that will stand on its own. Use collage and paper sculpture techniques with construction paper, textured papers, oil pastels, colored markers, and/or paint to create panels for each of the four seasons. If desired, write a haiku or other poem about each season and attach to the back of the screen.

- As a class, make a paper collage "quilt" that features a local or regional biome/ecosystem at different seasons throughout the year. Brainstorm to encourage discussion and create a list of possible local scenes or events to be depicted. Each student should complete a 9-in. or 12-in. quilt square using collage techniques and colored construction paper. Details and signatures can be added with colored markers if desired. The completed blocks may be glued edge to edge on large sheets of butcher paper, or joined with narrow strips of colored paper to make a paper quilt.

- Create a torn paper landscape of a specific local or regional biome/ecosystem that includes a foreground, middle ground, and background. On white 12 x 18-in. paper (turned either horizontally or vertically), mark with pencil or colored chalk a horizon line high on the paper, another line across the middle, and a foreground line near the bottom of the paper. Select three different colors of construction paper in light, medium, and dark values. Starting with the darkest color, tear one edge. Place along the horizon line (with the straight edge parallel to the white paper's bottom edge) and glue in place. Repeat the process for the middle shade and lightest shade, overlapping so that the lightest color's straight edge is aligned with the bottom of the white paper. Glue each piece in place. Use scrap construction paper and markers, oil pastels, or crayons to create details in the landscape. Include overlapping objects to indicate depth and include some evidence of humanity and its effect on the environment.

- Paint a tempera resist landscape depicting a seasonal scene of a specific biome/ecosystem. Tempera resist uses the resist properties of a water-based ink and a nonsoluble mixture of tempera paint and glue to produce striking results. The colored areas of the finished painting will appear subtly shaded and outlined in black and a dramatic visual contrast will be evident between the reflective painted surface and the matte-black inked areas. Begin by drawing the subject in pencil on a piece of heavy watercolor paper. Thickly paint the areas of the work to be colored with a mixture of half-liquid tempera paint and half-white glue.

  Colors may be mixed with the glue in palettes or small cups, but only in amounts that will be needed for one sitting. Wash palettes, cups, and brushes thoroughly at the end of each session. When painting, leave the lines of the drawing and any areas intended to be black unpainted. These areas of unpainted paper will absorb the black ink, while the painted areas will resist it. Any areas that are intended as snow must be painted white. When painting is complete, let dry, then cover it with a thin coat of undiluted black ink and let dry completely. Using a soft brush, wet one area of the painting at a time and gently rinse away ink from the painted areas.

- Locate newspaper accounts of local, national, or international natural disasters (tornadoes, hurricanes, floods, fires, etc.) and choose one to use as a subject for a narrative painting or mixed media work of art. If desired, include actual newspaper clippings, magazine articles, and text.

- As a class, design and paint a large, collaborative mural in your school that depicts your biome/ecosystem and its physical characteristics, including natural disasters and other kinds of weather (secure permission to paint on the wall first). After choosing the subject of the mural, draw sketches for all or part of the mural. Assemble all sketches and organize in a final design that is in scale with the wall to be painted. Divide responsibilities among class members. Prepare the wall by cleaning and painting it with a base coat, enlarge and transfer the design, paint major areas, and then add final details. If possible, unveil the completed mural with a dedication ceremony at the school.

- Early geological surveys included artists and photographers who traveled with the exploring and mapmaking expeditions to visually record what they discovered. These illustrations often were included in reports to Congress and other governmental entities. Imagine that you are an artist accompanying such an expedition and create a travel diary that includes sketches, watercolor paintings, and notes. To choose a destination, research the U.S. Geological Survey Fact Sheets and topographic maps available on the Internet.

- Biosphere 2 is a 7,200,000 cubic foot sealed glass and space frame structure in Arizona that contains elements from Earth (Biosphere 1). Inside the living laboratory are seven wilderness ecosystems, including a rainforest and a 900,000 gallon ocean, as well as a human habitat. Take a virtual tour of Biosphere 2 available at http://www.bio2.edu. After researching the project, create a model of a new biosphere for the planet Mars.

Printmaking with Subjects from the Natural World

The Scientific Method and Art Criticism

Color Theory

Timeline of Art Materials

The Chemistry of Ceramics

Symmetry in Science

Natural Science: Landscapes and Biomes

Printmaking with Subjects from the Natural World

The Rainforest Biome

Scientific Illustration

Metamorphosis

Botanical Field Journals

Photo by Nancy Walkup

Printmaking with Subjects from the Natural World

Though the methods for foam board and linoleum block printing are similar, it is recommended, for safety reasons, that elementary students use only foam board, though secondary students may use either foam board or linoleum block for printing.

Foam Board Printmaking

Make foam board prints that depict figures in a natural landscape. Begin by drawing a line design in pencil on newsprint cut the same size as the foam board printing plate that will be used. The drawing should fill the space, but the lines of the design should not be too close together or too detailed. Using masking tape, attach the drawing, image side up, to the foam board printing plate. Trace over the image lightly with a dull pencil to transfer the drawing to the board. Remove the newsprint and trace over the lines on the foam board again with a dull pencil. The lines created in the foam board need to be fairly deep to print well, but care should be taken that the pencil does not cut through the board.

Place the foam board faceup on a stack of newspaper. Squeeze or spoon out a line of printing ink on a printing tray and roll a brayer in the ink to coat it evenly. Roll the ink-covered brayer over the foam board print plate. Roll in several directions, paying particular attention to the edges of the block. Place the inked plate faceup on a clean piece of newspaper. Press printing paper right side down over the block and rub evenly with hands or brayer. Carefully pull off the print from one end and hang to dry. Repeat the entire process to print an edition (the plate must be reinked for each new print). Number, sign, and title the prints when dry. If desired, have students each write about the meaning of one or more of their prints and display the narratives alongside the prints.

Linoleum Block Printmaking

Create a linoleum block print of a specific local or regional biome/ecosystem. Begin with a line drawing on newsprint that is the same size as the printing block that will be used. The drawing should fill the space, but lines should not be too close together or too detailed. Shade the back of the design with heavy pencil, then tape the finished drawing to the printing block, image side up, with small pieces of masking tape. Trace over the image with a pencil (this transfers the image to the print block). Remove the newsprint paper and use a linoleum cutter to carve into the block along the lines of the transferred drawing.

To print, place the block faceup on a stack of newspaper. Squeeze or spoon out a line of printing ink on a printing tray and roll a brayer in the ink to coat it evenly. Roll the ink-covered brayer over the print block. Roll in several directions, paying particular attention to the edges of the block. Place the inked block faceup on a clean piece of newspaper. Press printing paper right side down over the block and rub evenly with hands or brayer. Carefully pull off the print from one end and hang to dry. Repeat the entire process to print an edition (the plate must be reinked for each new print). Number, sign, and title the prints when dry. If desired, handmade or marbleized paper could be made for the prints.

Gyotaku: Japanese Fish Printing

Gyotaku (guh-yo-tah-koo) is Japanese for "fish print." An actual fish is inked and placed on paper or cloth, where it leaves an image of itself, complete with eyes, scales, fins, and gills. It is a relatively new technique, originating about 100 years ago as a way for Japanese fishermen to record the exact size and kind of fish they had caught. Sometimes gyotaku are displayed on the walls of homes, or sometimes they are kept in a journal to document a successful fishing spot. Japanese fishing magazines hold yearly contests for the largest fish caught; judging is done from the gyotaku.

Fishermen in the United States sometimes exaggerate the size of the fish they have caught or let go. In Japan, the gyotaku provides an accurate record of the catch. In addition, the print is a work of art, to be hung on the wall and admired, not only for the size of the fish, but for the aesthetic appeal of the print. The Western fisherman might have his or her fish mounted and hung on the wall to be admired, but it is not a work of art. Also, when fish are prepared in this way by a taxidermist, the meat cannot be eaten. After the Japanese fisherman records his fish as a gyotaku, he can take the fish home and eat it. What cultural differences can be discerned from these practices?

There are two methods of printing from a fish. The indirect method (kansetsu-ho) involves molding wet paper directly onto the fish, carefully tamping it down so that it will pick up all the details, pulling it off and then letting it dry. The paper itself then becomes the plate. The second method is called chokusetsu-ho. It is faster and easier to make multiple images with this technique. First, the fish must be fresh, clean, and dry (frozen fish may also be used). Remove the slimy residue from the fish's scales with salt, vinegar, or alcohol. Lay the fish on a flat surface and gently fan out the fins and tail. Lumps of plasticene clay can be placed under the fins and tail to elevate them. Apply

watercolor, sumi ink, or water-based printing inks directly to the fish with a soft brush, sponge, or foam brayer. Finally, place a sheet of paper over the inked fish. Hold the paper with one hand at the fish's middle section. With the other hand, gently press the paper so that it comes into contact with the entire inked surface, especially the fins and tail. Then peel back the paper to reveal a mirror image of the fish. Note: Gyotaku may also be done on fabric, using fabric paints instead of water-based paints.

Nasco makes rubber fish replicas for gyotaku. This allows teachers to bypass the issues of availability, preparation, and perishability of real fish in the classroom. Aesthetically speaking, is the rubber fish a valid substitute for a fresh fish when making an art print? Would the experience of printing with a rubber fish give as much insight into the culture of the Japanese people and their artwork? Many teachers would not try gyotaku because of the smell and mess of the fish. In this case, would it be better to substitute a rubber fish, or just not do it at all?

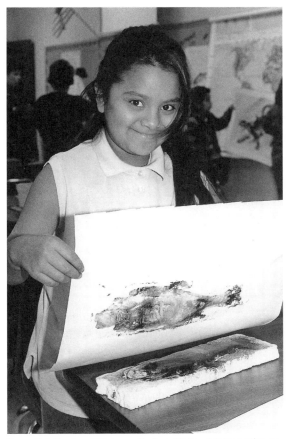

Nasco Fish Replicas, 901 Janesville Ave., P.O. Box 901, Fort Atkinson, Wisconsin 53538-0901; 800-558-9595. Photo by Nancy Walkup.

The Rainforest Biome

The Scientific Method and Art Criticism

Color Theory

Timeline of Art Materials

The Chemistry of Ceramics

Symmetry in Science

Natural Science: Landscapes and Biomes

Printmaking with Subjects from the Natural World

The Rainforest Biome

Scientific Illustration

Metamorphosis

Botanical Field Journals

Photo by Nancy Walkup.

Rainforest Biome Activities

▶ Design and create a paper sculpture rainforest or other chosen natural environment. Direct groups of students to make a painted or collaged background on large sheets of paper taped over selected walls and to construct three-dimensional trees, vines, bushes, flowers, and other vegetation, and animals, reptiles, and birds. Paper sculpture and papier mâché techniques may be used as desired. Assemble the environment when its components are complete.

▶ Create an artwork that depicts a rainforest animal, insect, bird, or reptile hidden through camouflage. Begin by finding photographs in nature magazines of animals, insects, or reptiles from the rainforest. Choose one of the pictures and carefully cut out the creature from the background so that only the chosen subject remains. Glue the picture on a similar color of construction paper, and then create an environment in which your subject will be hidden by camouflage. Use tempera colors to either blend the animal into the background or use combinations of color, shape, and/or behavior to help it appear hidden in its environment.

▶ Pretend that you are a biologist on an expedition to the rainforest. Develop a field journal of the expedition, including a detailed account of your experiences along with field notes and drawings of the flora and fauna you encounter.

▶ Photograph or find a picture of plants and birds native to the rainforest or to your own biome/ecosystem. Draw a grid over the picture, and then use the grid as a visual aid to enlarge the image to a much larger size. Paint the enlarged image with watercolors or acrylics.

▶ Research tropical or local plants, birds, and animals, then choose one to commemorate in a postage stamp promoting environmental awareness. Create your design in both a large format and stamp size, displaying the two together, much as a graphic artist would do for an actual stamp competition. Choose art media from acrylics, watercolors, or colored markers.

▶ Imagine that you are in the rainforest with an expedition and have discovered a previously unknown species of tropical bird. Paint a watercolor of the newly discovered bird that also includes detailed, close-up sketches of its unusual characteristics. Create a name for the bird and include field notes with your painting (for example, detail the environment where the bird was sighted, its size and description, and behavior observed).

Suggested Artists and Artworks

▶ Alfredo Arrequin, *Sueno (Dream: Eve Before Adam)*

▶ David Bates, *Night Heron,* or other works about the swamp

▶ Martin Johnson Heade, *Cattleya Orchid and Three Brazilian Hummingbirds*

▶ Maria Sibylla Merian, *Flowers, Butterflies, and Insects*

Scientific Illustration

Scientific Illustration: The Artist/Naturalist

"Art is hidden in nature and he who can draw it out possesses it."

—Albrecht Durer

Many illustrations that depict scientific concepts, natural objects, and living things can be found in science and biology textbooks. These images are created by scientific illustrators, artists with special interests and skills in one or more areas of science. Scientific illustrators may specialize in natural sciences such as medical or botanical illustration, but individually they must have a strong scientific curiosity and a keen interest in both art and science. They must be expert at seeing detail and drawing accurately what they observe. Scientific or medical illustrators are usually accomplished in many media and techniques. They work closely with doctors and scientists to accurately create drawings, paintings, and models for publication in textbooks, identification manuals, and other science-based publications. Through their "double vision," scientific illustrators view the natural world through the double perspectives of art and science.

Suggested Artists/Naturalists and Artworks

- John James Audubon, *Birds of America* and *Mammals of America*
- David Bates
- Basil Besler
- George Brookshaw
- Albrecht Durer, *The Large Turf* or *A Great Piece of Turf*, 1503
- John Gould
- Martin Johnson Heade
- Maria Sibylla Merian, *Metamorphosis Insectorum Surinamensium*, 1705
- Georgia O'Keeffe, many flower images
- Pierre-Joseph Redoute
- Robert Thornton
- Vincent van Gogh, many flower images

Artists Who Pioneered the Study of Anatomy for Art

Leonardo da Vinci, Vitruvian Man (also see Geoman at http://www.geoman.com/geoman.html)

Rembrandt, Anatomical Lecture, 1632

Andreas Vesalius, On the Structure of the Human Body, 1543

Resources

Blunt, Wilfrid. *The Art of Botanical Illustration: An Illustrated History.* New York: Dover, 1994.

James, John, Brown, Colin, and Walker, Cyril. *Audubon: American Birds.* New York: Random House, 1999.

Kramer, Jack. *Women of Flowers: A Tribute to Victorian Women Illustrators.* Stewart Tabori & Chang, 1996.

Merian, Maria Sibylla. *Flowers, Butterflies and Insects.* New York: Dover Publications, 1991.

West, Keith. R. *How to Draw Plants: The Techniques of Botanical Illustration.* Timber Press, 1996.

Internet Resource

Botany Information Sources, http://www.nhm.ac.uk/info/links/bot.htm

Metamorphosis

Student Reading: Metamorphosis and the Botanical Artist Maria Sibylla Merian

Metamorphosis

Artists have been particularly adept at illustrating the biological process of metamorphosis—a change or transformation through distinct stages in the life cycles of living things. For example, insects hatch from eggs, then molt or shed their exoskeletons or skins as they grow larger. Changes in insect forms may occur with each successive molt. In simple metamorphosis, insects develop from egg to larva, then adult, but the larva resembles the adult. In complete metamorphosis, for instance, in butterflies and moths, development proceeds through a series of complete transformations through egg to larva (caterpillar), to pupa (chrysalis or cocoon), to winged adult.

Maria Sibylla Merian

Maria Sibylla Merian (1647-1717) was one of the great female artists of the 17th century. Her work depicts a particular sensitivity toward the natural world and its inhabitants. Merian was the first person, man or woman, to create a scientific record chronicling the biological process of metamorphosis—the transformation through distinct stages in the life cycles of living things. Her pioneering artwork cast light on these mysterious transformations of insects and plants as they develop. Much of her research took place in the dense forests of the Dutch colony of Surinam on the north coast of South America, a difficult prospect for any woman at the time.

In 1997, the U.S. Postal Service issued two botanical prints stamps featuring two illustrations by Merian. The stamps feature a flowering pineapple with two varieties of cockroaches and a citron pictured with moth, larva, pupa, and beetle. The subjects were selected from more than 70 Merian engravings housed at the National Museum of Women in the Arts.

▸ Research Merian on the National Museum of Women in the Arts website (www.nmwa.edu). Look for contemporary botanical artists online and compare their work to Merian's.

▸ Why was Merian so unique as an artist? As a woman?

▸ Research a particular species of butterfly or moth, then depict its different stages of complete metamorphosis in a black and white line drawing.

Internet Resources

http://www.nmwa.org/legacy/bios/bmerian.htm

http://cgee.hamline.edu/see/mariasyblla/see_an_merian.html

Botanical Field Journals

Through field journals, the relationship between art and science can be investigated firsthand. Students can learn to see as an artist sees, emphasizing details that seem most important. They can depict the shape, color, line, and symmetry or asymmetry of individual plants, making both written, narrative notes and sketches in a field journal. Students can work both independently and collaboratively, calling on other students to confirm their findings, and comparing and contrasting their discoveries with each other. Creating a field journal helps students become more aware of the natural environment around them. Students will engage in activities typical of professional botanists or other natural scientists. In the tradition of botanical illustration, students will include the flower, fruit, leaf, stalk, and seed of plants in their artwork.

Activities

▸ Obtain or create field journals. Unlined notebooks can be used for field journals or journals can be made by assembling copies of the following handout, "Field Journal Page." Recycled paper or handmade paper made with natural materials are other options. The size, length, and complexity of the journal are adaptable to student needs.

▸ Invite local botanists or botanical artists to class to discuss how they work.

▸ Visit botanical gardens, natural history centers, or zoos and record observations in the field journal.

▸ Encourage students to be creative with their journals to make them aesthetically pleasing as well as scientifically accurate. If possible, show examples of actual field journals.

▸ Vary the media and techniques used. Black and white line drawings or watercolor paintings are standards for artist/botanists, but other media can be used. Botanical images are effective through relief printmaking, scratchboard, three-dimensional paper sculptures, sculptures made with found materials, low-relief sculptures made from clay, or clay tiles.

▸ Create drawings to scale; for example, a drawing could be $1/2$ scale to the actual size of the plant, such as 1 inch = 2 inch.

▸ Using plant specimens brought into class, draw plants from direct observation in a field journal or on drawing paper. Include descriptive and narrative notes about the plants and illustrations. Identify and label the parts of the plants.

▸ Conduct research using field guides, books, journals, or web sites to select plants as subjects for extended reports with more elaborate illustrations. Limiting choices to plants native to the region will make securing actual specimens more likely. Create a presentation that includes both written and illustrated components.

▸ Prepare an illustrated or multimedia presentation on a noted artist/botanist.

▸ Use plant specimens from florists or grown at home as subjects.

▸ Use vegetable plants as plant specimens. Grow plants such as beans or potatoes in class for purposes of observation and drawing.

▸ Use the research on Maria Sibylla Merian as background information to create botanical postage stamp designs. Find and discuss other examples of stamps that depict nature.

▸ Following Merian's example, create a botanical drawing that includes the stages of metamorphosis. The drawing could include only plants or the addition of insects or birds.

▸ Research local plant life to compare life cycles with the seasons. Draw the same plant four times, depicting how it changes with each season.

Field Journal Page

Name _____

Date _____

Time _____

Temperature/Weather Conditions _____

_____

Location _____

Comments/Details:

_____

_____

_____

_____

_____

_____

_____

_____

_____

_____

_____

Please draw your field sketches on the back of this page if extra room is needed.

Chapter 7
Art and Social Studies

"*History provides the setting and context for a work of art and helps us understand the artist and the circumstances in which the work was made. Artworks reflect the times and cultures of the people who produced them. Art history provides a kind of timeline that shows how art has developed from early human history to the present. It also shows how artists have been influenced by previous artistic styles, by technology and social change and the like, and how these influences showed up in their artwork . . . . We understand today's art more fully when we can trace its development through time.*"

— Gerald Brommer, *Discovering Art History*

Art and Social Studies

Look in any social studies textbook and you will find reproductions of works of art — paintings and other works that tell stories of the past in visual form. Artists and photographers have captured both momentous and less important events of their time and made them accessible through the universal language of art. Through investigations of historical artworks, we can share in emotional dramas of the past, investigate different perspectives on historical events, explore the context of historical artworks, and compare the past with the present.

Historians and social scientists investigate how people live today or in the past. Much of their investigations are guided by clues that they gather from objects or artifacts that people use or from written historical documents. Often these objects are considered to be works of art and they, too, can also tell about the ways that people live and think. Learning about the ways that people from other times, places, and cultures live and think helps everyone better understand and respect each other's customs and traditions. Since art is such a part of the culture that produces it, any study of art without inclusion of its cultural context would be sadly lacking.

Art and Social Studies

Art and Culture

One of the standards in the National Council for Social Studies Standards addresses the issue of culture: "Explain and give examples of how language, literature, the arts, architecture, other artifacts, traditions, beliefs, values, and behaviors contribute to the development and transmission of culture." As works of art reflect the cultures in which they are produced, art presents an effective medium through which to study culture. The visual language of art provides access to the interpretation of ideas, values, and concerns from cultures both contemporary and historic, even without the knowledge of a language.

An art-centered approach to social studies promotes a wider, more inclusive definition of art that recognizes and celebrates cultural diversity. A work of art from any culture and time period can be studied through an examination of universal concepts, themes, and issues. In order to provide multiple views of what defines an object as "art," it is important to include in the curriculum folk art, popular art, artifacts, crafts and functional items, as well as "fine art."

In Practice

Three or four different works of art may be sufficient for comparison of specific themes, important social issues, or world views of art, depending on lesson or unit objectives and availability of resources. Teachers might want to consider social studies themes based on human commonalities such as communication, work, structures, or time. Art forms, folklore, and mythology offer other ways to approach the study of cultures.

Art Historians, Museums, and Technology

The development of museums some two hundred years ago first allowed the general public to view art. Today in a single afternoon in a museum we can experience a wide range of objects from different times and places. This increased access to art has also influenced art historians.

A wide variety of technological advances has provided easy access to images. Development of mass printing and the ability to reproduce images photographically revolutionized the discipline. In our time, electronic images on the computer allow a vast new public the opportunity to experience works of art while also raising new concerns about copyright and reproduction rights.

Correlating Art, Art History, and Social Studies

In *Art History and Education*, Stephen Addiss and Mary Erickson suggest that art history offers:

"*The chance to participate in the entire world of artistic expression: from prehistoric times to the present day, and from Africa, Asia, and Europe to our own towns, schools, and homes. In the process, we will also discover that art history can be one of the most exciting ways to investigate the cultures of the world and their histories ... ... As artworks from around the world serve as vehicles to understanding, art historical studies can help students begin to develop as students of the world.*"

In elementary and secondary schools, art history provides natural correlations to social studies. Concepts of culture, historical events, chronology, geography, and the use of timelines and maps are shared by both disciplines. By approaching the study of art history and social studies through works of art, students can:

▶ discuss and interpret visuals

▶ compare cultures of the world

▶ identify contributions of various cultures, past and present, to world civilizations

▶ identify basic institutions common to all cultures

▶ respect beliefs of other individuals, groups, and cultures

▶ describe changes over time

▶ differentiate between fact and fiction

▶ make and interpret timelines

▶ sequence events on timelines and chronologies

▶ locate and gather information in reference works

▶ locate geographic sites on world globes and maps

▶ compare and contrast opposing viewpoints

▶ organize and express ideas in written form

▶ analyze information and draw conclusions

▶ develop criteria for making judgments

Resources

Tchertok, Bobbi, Hirshfield, Goody, and Rosh, Marilyn. *Teaching American History with Art Masterpieces.* New York: Scholastic Professional Books, 1998.

Be a Historian or Social Scientist

Photo by Nancy Walkup

Be a Historian or Social Scientist

"The past is intelligible to us only in the light of the present; and we can fully understand the present only in the light of the past."

— Edward Hallet Carr, Historian

To demonstrate what a social scientist or historian does, ask students to think about the description that a historian or social scientist would write about the students, the classroom, and objects used in the classroom. What do these objects tell about the time, place, and society of the classroom?

Place students in small collaborative groups. Provide an image to each group. Instruct students to look closely at the artwork and to consider it as a document about a time, place, and culture. Answer the following questions and provide one or more supporting reasons for each response.

- ▶ Where is the place?
- ▶ What is happening?
- ▶ Why is the event happening?
- ▶ When in history does the scene happen?
- ▶ Who is the main character or who are the main characters?
- ▶ What does this artwork tell you about the culture or society that created it?

Art timelines help students visualize chronological order. Sequential placement of art objects on a timeline can effectively demonstrate many concepts such as:

- ▶ How art media and techniques have changed over time.
- ▶ How art materials have changed through history.
- ▶ How styles change from one time to another.
- ▶ Which artists are contemporaries and which artists worked in different times.

Using Primary Sources in Social Studies and Art

Courtesy Amon Carter Museum. Photo by Nancy Walkup.

Primary Sources

For historians, the most significant historical evidence is a primary resource, any uninterpreted source of information. The use of primary resources such as letters, diaries, first person accounts, and visual images such as photographs and artworks, helps make both social studies and art concepts more meaningful to students. Working directly with primary sources helps students ask probing questions, think critically, and develop reasoned explanations and interpretations of events and issues in the past and present. Students can interpret primary sources, just as they can make reasoned interpretations of works of art.

Secondary Sources

Secondary sources are interpretations of events of the past written or created by people writing or making art about events after they happened. A history textbook is one example of a secondary source.

Five types of primary sources include:

1. Objects such as artifacts, tools, inventions, clothing, sculpture and other three-dimensional forms of art
2. Images such as artworks, photographs, film, video, and maps
3. Audio such as oral histories, interviews, and music
4. Statistics such as land surveys, maps, blueprints, or architectural drawings
5. Text in the form of documents, such as diaries, memoirs, and manuscripts

Choosing Primary Resources

Choose Meaningful Primary Sources that:

▶ present a puzzle;

▶ challenge a stereotype or conventional wisdom;

▶ offer an insight (or experience);

▶ promote empathy (through a human interest story); or

▶ present an explanation.

Using Primary Sources in Social Studies and Art

Activities

▸ Use online and library research to discover primary sources.

▸ Use contemporary primary sources to focus instruction on a historical period or, conversely, use a historical primary source to focus inquiry on a contemporary issue.

▸ Read and write immediate reactions to a thought-provoking document, and then compare differences in student responses through class discussion.

▸ Select primary source images to create a museum display about an historical period and write gallery cards to accompany the images.

▸ Write a response to a primary source, taking the point of view of someone who lived at the time the source was created.

▸ Make an illustrated timeline based on primary resources.

▸ Identify and discover the use of unknown objects or objects pictured in an old photograph.

▸ Use historic photographs as a focus to learn more about the context in which they were taken.

▸ Compare historic photographs with contemporary ones of the same themes or subjects.

▸ Explore the meaning and context of fine art, first looking for visual clues in the work, then conducting research in reference books or online to discover more about when and why they were created.

▸ Focus on an artifact that is both functional and visually pleasing. Decide if it would be most appropriately placed in an art or a historical museum. Provide reasons for the choice.

▸ Research your family history by interviewing older relatives. Use letters, artwork, audio recordings, or videotape to compile a report on an important story or event in your family.

▸ Research, design, and create an artistic family tree with text and illustrations.

▸ Research and study lyrics of popular songs from a range of time periods. How do they reflect events that were happening at that time?

▸ Compare and contrast visual art with music in the same time period.

▸ Listen to audio recordings of famous speeches and old radio broadcasts and compare their differences to television today.

▸ Find the locations of primary resource origins on a map or globe.

▸ Interpret historical maps and compare them to contemporary versions of the same locality.

▸ Create an illustrated map of the school neighborhood, community, or city.

▸ Conduct research on recipes from historic cookbooks and compare them to recipes found today for the same food. Choose a recipe, illustrate it, and then actually cook it.

▸ Use old catalog pages or newspaper ads to research fashion trends, household articles, cost of living, and lifestyles of a particular period. How do they compare to similar items in contemporary catalogs and newspapers? How have they changed?

▸ Discuss how packaging design influences consumers. Choose a product or food item and create an illustrated ad or packaging design (such as a cereal box) for it.

▸ Read and discuss diaries and firsthand accounts of historical events, such as the Diary of Anne Frank. Make an illustration depicting an event in the text.

▸ Read and consider letters from a particular time period. Assume a persona and write an illustrated letter from that point of view. The illustrated letters of the Western artist Charles Russell provide great examples for this activity. *Cowboy Charlie: The Story of Charles M. Russell* by Jeanette Winter, 1995, is recommended for elementary students and *Charles M. Russell, Word Painter; Letters, 1887-1926*, 1993, is appropriate for all ages.

▸ Explore how illustrations complement the text in books and magazines.

▸ Investigate family photographs, memorabilia, recipes, clothing or jewelry, and oral histories to discover family stories about them. Create an original scrapbook to visually tell and record the stories.

▸ Research customs, language, dress, foods, and cultural traditions of your ancestral country or countries. Create a collage that incorporates what is learned.

▸ Research the history of historically or architecturally significant buildings in your community. Visit and photograph the buildings with a digital camera and then compare the photographs with historical photos of the same structures. Publish the photos and research findings online.

▸ Create and distribute an illustrated brochure of a walking tour of the significant buildings in the downtown of your area.

Using Primary Sources in Social Studies and Art: Interpreting Works of Art in Context

Answer the following questions about a work of art.

Title and Date of Artwork: _____

Artist: _____

Describe in detail how the artwork looks.

What clues can you find about the time in which it was produced?

What clues can you find about the culture in which it was produced?

What is it made of?

How was it made?

What was its function or purpose?

What is the history of the object itself? Who owns it now? Who owned it in the past?

What story does it tell?

What meaning does it express for you?

Using Primary Sources in Social Studies and Art: Interpreting an Historical Photograph

Answer the following questions about a historical photograph.

Name _____

Title and Date of Photograph _____

Photographer _____

What is the subject of the photograph?

What is the setting for the photograph?

When and where in the past do you think the photograph was taken? How can you tell?

What story do you think is being told?

What meaning does the photograph reveal about its subject?

What is the photographer's point of view?

Could this photograph be considered as a work of art? Give reasons for your answer.

Using Primary Sources in Social Studies and Art: Thinking Like a Museum Curator

In a museum, a curator is an expert, usually with special knowledge of a particular type of art or time period. Curators often choose works for an exhibition and write the descriptions or explanations that are placed on the wall in the museum beside each corresponding work.

Choose five artworks (primary sources) to create a museum display about a historical topic. Name the exhibit and write gallery cards to accompany each work.

Title of Exhibit _____

Title _____

Artist _____

Date _____

Text for Gallery Card

Title _____

Artist _____

Date _____

Text for Gallery Card

Title _____

Artist _____

Date _____

Text for Gallery Card

Title _____

Artist _____

Date _____

Text for Gallery Card

Title _____

Artist _____

Date _____

Text for Gallery Card

Using Primary Sources in Social Studies and Art

Additional Activities

▸ Research, write, and illustrate a newspaper page that describes local, state, national and international events on your date of birth.

▸ Choose a contemporary scene of street life that represents social issues of today. Create a painting, drawing, or collage based on the chosen theme, using only a pair of complementary colors (red/green, blue/orange, or yellow/violet) and black and white.

▸ Assemble a still life with agricultural products from your geographic region of the country. Use colored construction paper, scissors, and glue to create a collage based on the still life. Add details with crayons or markers.

▸ Compare and contrast paintings that depict agriculture and land resources. Possibilities include *Fall Plowing, Spring Turning, Spring in Town*, and *Breaking the Prairie Sod* by Grant Wood; *Tornado over Kansas* by John Steuart Curry; and *Threshing Wheat* and *The White Calf* by Thomas Hart Benton. These three artists popularized the American art movement known as Regionalism. Regionalist paintings celebrated the simple, basic values of the heartland of America and proved that the life and values of rural America were worthy as subjects of art. Look in the paintings for evidence of the four types of resources: land, labor, capital goods, and entrepreneurship. Also determine and compare the artists' use of points of view: normal eye view, worm's eye view, or bird's eye view.

▸ Create a landscape that depicts specific land resources or agriculture of your region. Painting, drawing, collage, or mixed media would all be appropriate for this activity.

▸ Choose a contemporary profession or industry and create a drawing or painting that depicts people working together in an appropriate setting. This can be an individual project or a mural developed collaboratively by a small group or an entire class. Related artworks include *Builders* by Jacob Lawrence and *Detroit Industry* by Diego Rivera.

▸ Using found objects, design and assemble an imaginary, three-dimensional "tool" such as a homework machine or other laborsaving device.

▸ Think about symbols that represent different professions—for example, an apple for a teacher, a hammer for a carpenter, or a paintbrush for an artist. Choose a symbol to represent a specific profession. Incorporate the symbol into a design for a foam board or linoleum cut print.

▸ Choose a family or community recreational activity that provides opportunities to directly purchase food or other items (for example, a state fair, arts festival, rodeo, amusement park, Popsicle truck, snow cone or lemonade stand, roadside fruit and vegetable market). Illustrate the chosen subject through a painting, collage, or three-dimensional diorama. *The Fair at Reynosa/La Feria en Reynosa* by Carmen Lomas Garza is a related artwork by an artist who illustrates and writes bilingual children's books, such as *Family Pictures/Cuadros de Familia* and *In My Family/En mi Familia*.

▸ Choose a meaningful or humorous childhood memory of a family outing or activity to illustrate, especially one in which food plays a part. Drawing, painting, collage, or sculpture are all adaptable as media for this activity.

▸ Identify and research local historical murals, then work in teams to design and create a mural at your school.

Richard Haas, *The Chisholm Trail Cattledrive*, Fort Worth, Texas. Photo by Nancy Walkup.

Introduction to Timelines and Chronologies

Photo by Nancy Walkup.

Introduction to Timelines and Chronologies

Sequencing art images by means of a timeline is a practical, easy, and fun method to encourage students to think about natural and logical connections between art and social studies and other subjects as well. Formats and complexity of timelines are easily adaptable for use with many grade levels of students. Timeline activities can be as simple as sequencing postcards of animals or as complex as a hyperlinked, online publication. Commercially available timelines, chronologies, historical compilations, and the Internet provide great resources for developing timelines.

Resources

Create-A-Timeline, Crystal Productions, 1992.

Gottlieb, Agnes, Gottlieb, Henry, Bowers, Barbara, and Bowers, Brent. *1000 Years, 1000 People: Ranking the Men and Women Who Shaped the Millennium*. New York: Kodansha America, 1998.

Grun, Bernard. *The Timetables of History: A Horizontal Linkage of People and Events*. New York: Simon & Schuster: 1991.

Hellemans, Alexander, and Bunch, Bryan. *The Timetables of Science: A Chronology of the Most Important People and Events in the History of Science*. New York: Simon & Schuster: 1991.

Stewart, Robert. *Ideas that Shaped Our World*. San Diego: Thunder Bay Press, 1997.

Approaches to Timelines

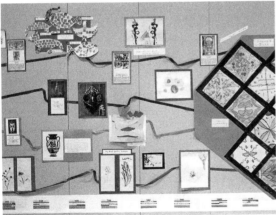

Photo by Nancy Walkup.

Postcard Timelines

▸ Gather postcards that represent different times and cultures. Postcards work well because they usually include information such as artist, title, and dates. Use masking tape to create a simple timeline across several tables or on the floor. At one end of the tape write "Now." At the other end write "Then." (Another option is to write "Old, Older, Oldest.") Have students place images on the timeline in the order they think they were created. What clues helped students place the images?

▸ Use the masking tape timeline to place art postcards or study prints in an order that shows a sequential chronology of the events depicted in the images. Use the dates on the backs of the postcards or prints to arrange them chronologically. What observations and conclusions can students propose about how the art changed over time? Were any of the findings surprising?

▸ Stretch a piece of masking tape across the floor or a long table. Divide the line into time divisions (decades, half-centuries, centuries). Distribute postcards or other small art images to the students. Ask students not to look at the date on the back of the postcard. Ask students to decide where on the timeline their image(s) might fit. When all images are placed on the timeline, have the class look at the sequence of placement. Do any artworks appear out of sequence? Can the students infer why? Why did each student place his/her image where he/she did? Turn over any questionably placed images and determine proper placement.

Other approaches include classifying art objects by type (three-dimensional, two-dimensional, realistic, abstract), contrasting and comparing different styles, or predicting future styles.

Pocketed Timeline

▸ Purchase library card pockets from a school supply catalog and mount them horizontally on long strips of poster or other strong board glued together to make a long strip. With a marker, label each pocket in increments of 50-100 years. Provide students with art postcards and ask them to place them in the pockets where they think they belong (ask them not to look on the back of the cards). This can be an ongoing class activity throughout the year.

Timeline in a Can

▸ Open and empty a coffee or other kind of can, then wash it thoroughly. Glue a long strip of paper (such as an adding machine roll of paper) or thin plastic that can be rolled into the can.

Using a permanent marker, mark the strip into increments of 50-100 years. The timeline can be rolled, stored, and transported in the can. As described above, the timeline can be laid out flat when needed for use. Art images could also be added as student drawings or small pictures cut from magazines or catalogs.

Interdisciplinary Timeline

This sample format can be adapted to different needs and purposes, but it provides a graphic organizer or chart to compile interdisciplinary connections across time and disciplines. To use the diagram, choose a theme and periods of time. Write in the appropriate dates or years vertically in the first column then conduct research to find connections to the theme from each subject area.

Timeline Theme: _____

Date/Year	Art	Social Studies	Language Arts	Science	Mathematics

Art and Social Studies Chronology

Use this chart to record the names and dates of works of arts and events that happened at the same time in history. Provide an explanation about each entry.

List Title, Artist, and Date for each Artwork	List Important Events Taking Place at the Same Time

Sequencing Art History with Postcards

Sequencing Art History with Postcards

Assemble sets of art postcards in resealable plastic bags, one set for each small group of four or five students. Each set should contain an assortment of different artworks from varied cultures and times. Include subject matter such as people, places, things, and ideas, and works representative of realistic, abstract, and nonobjective art.

Directions

▶ Have students sit in small groups at tables, if possible. Give each group a set of cards and ask them to remove the postcards from the bag and lay all the cards face up on the table.

▶ Tell students they are not to read the back of the cards just yet. Ask the groups to work together to line up their cards from the oldest to the most recent, solely by looking at the images and making reasoned judgments as to their chronological sequence. When students complete this task, ask them to now check the back of the cards for the dates and make any adjustments needed to correctly sequence the cards. Ask each group to briefly report on their experiences, explaining what they learned in the process.

▶ Have students again look carefully at the sequenced cards and discuss with the groups what changes they see in art over time.

Photo by Nancy Walkup.

Comparing and Contrasting Art and Social Studies Concepts

Choose an artwork to investigate from the alternative perspectives of art and social studies.

Title of Artwork: _____   Artist or Maker: _____

Art Concepts	**Social Studies Concepts**
(from the perspective of an art historian)	(from the perspective of a social scientist or historian)
How does the object/artifact look?	How does the object/artifact look?
For what was it used?	What was it used for?
For what culture was it created?	What culture was it created in?
In what time was it created?	In what time was it created?
What was happening in the art world at that time?	What events were happening in history at that time?
What would an art historian tell us about the culture that created it?	What would a historian tell us about the culture that created it?
Does it belong in an art museum or an anthropology museum?	Does it belong in an art museum or a history or anthropology museum?
What are your reasons for your choice?	What are your reasons for your choice?
Do you think this is more valuable as a work of art or as an historical artifact?	Do you think this is more valuable as a work of art or as an historical artifact?
Give reasons for your choice.	Give reasons for your choice.

Using Primary Sources in Social Studies and Art: Thinking Like a Museum Curator

Mind Mapping and Other Graphic Organizers

Photo by Nancy Walkup.

Mind or Concept Mapping

Mind or concept mapping is used in social studies and language arts as a graphic organizer for developing a central idea or theme in a nonlinear manner. The procedure was invented by Tony Buzan following his research on note-taking techniques. According to Buzan, mind mapping helps map knowledge in a way that helps people understand and remember new information, while using the whole brain and facilitating visual memory.

▶ To create a concept map, first identify a theme or overarching idea to use as your central word. Write the word or draw a picture of the idea in the middle of a piece of paper. Print words, rather than writing them in cursive. Work quickly and don't worry about your drawing skills.

▶ Next draw five to ten related main ideas as branches around the central idea (at least some of these should be artworks that meaningfully express the central theme). Write a single word or draw a picture on each branch to express an aspect of your main idea.

▶ As you brainstorm, connect subsidiary ideas with lines, arrows, or different colors to the center, leaving lots of space between concepts. Keep adding related ideas, words, and pictures on smaller branches. You might want to use different colors for each of your major branches. The completed concept map should look like a loose drawing with lines connected by pictures and words.

Other Graphic Organizers

Other graphic organizers useful for the study of art and social studies include Venn diagrams (see p. 27), a continuum used for timelines, semantic webbing, fishbone mapping, spider mapping, and clustering.

Resources

Bromley, Karen D'Angelo, Irwin-Devitis, Linda, and Modlo, Marcia. *Graphic Organizers: Visual Strategies for Active Learning*. Scholastic Trade, 1996.

Buzan, Tony, and Buzan, Barry. *The Mind Map Book: How to Use Radiant Thinking to Maximize Your Brain's Untapped Potential*. Plume, 1996.

Buzan, Tony. *Use Both Sides of Your Brain*. Dutton, 1991.

Parks, Sandra and Black, Howard. *Organizing Thinking: Book One: Graphic Organizers*. Critical Thinking Books, 1992.

Chapter 8
Promoting the Art Program

"*All our efforts at educational reform will be futile unless we make a commitment to effective, efficient, and relevant advocacy for the arts.*"

— MacArthur Goodwin, 1989

Art Advocacy

Underscoring the success of art advocacy are three factors:

▶ Persistence,

▶ Visibility, and

▶ Active participation of stakeholders.

Bringing quality art programs to schools requires a well-thought-out vision. From the onset, fundamental stakeholders such as the art teacher, parent groups, or other teachers, should make a clear statement of the goals and objectives of an art program. With these goals and objectives as guidelines, all efforts should then focus upon making them public. Taking the goals and objectives to a broader audience mandates determination and persistence. Grass roots advocacy efforts usually gain momentum through time, but stakeholders must be willing to try a variety of venues and be persistent in promotional strategies.

Making known the benefits of a comprehensive art education to the school community and the public can take many forms. Publications, exhibitions, and presentations provide substantial and diverse methods for reaching a wide audience and thereby making the art program visible.

Regardless of the type of promotions chosen — written, visual, or oral — advocacy for art education remains the fundamental responsibility of art teachers. For this reason, art teachers need to assume the public face of their programs and reach out to their peers, administrators, and the community for support. As the academic value of the art program becomes recognized, advocacy becomes less of a solitary effort by the art teacher and more a collaborative effort of stakeholders.

Rewards of art advocacy efforts can be considerable, with the payoff resulting in — among other benefits — stronger art programs, higher student enrollment, expanded staff, and facilities and larger budgets. The following advocacy activities have been successfully implemented in art departments across the United States.

Art Pins and Art Response Journal

Art Pins and Art Response Journal

Art Department Brochure

Art Department Newsletter

Exhibitions

Family Art Educational Evening

Art Pins and Art Response Journal

This activity — exploring an artwork and artist through journaling activities — is a good example of an activity with multiple applications. This activity can be easily used as an icebreaker with teachers or parents or as an integrated learning activity with students. Art pins for this activity are made from old art resource catalogs and mat board.

Directions for Use with Adult Groups

This activity is suggested for presentations to school boards, or for use in parent-teacher meetings or faculty meetings. If limited time is available for meeting with parents or other adults, prepare art pins and journals in advance and distribute these at the meeting. If ample time is provided, allow participants to create their own art pin.

To prepare the art pins:

▶ Carefully cut art images from old art resource catalogs.

▶ Cut mat board mounts so that a border of approximately $1/8$ to $1/4$ inch surrounds the art image.

▶ Using rubber cement, glue an image onto a mount and then smooth out any air bubbles or wrinkles.

▶ On the reverse side of the image, use hot glue adhesive to apply a pin back to the mount.

▶ Allow the image and pin back to dry.

▶ Make a copy of the art response journal (p. 130) for each participant.

▶ At the meeting, explain to participants that they are to wear an art pin and use the art response journal to record questions and comments — including their own — to the artwork on their pin.

▶ When participants have completed this part of the activity, provide time to discuss what they have learned about the art and artist or if their opinions about the artwork changed and why.

▶ Point out how the works of art stimulated communication among participants.

Art Pins and Art Response Journal

Directions for use with students

▶ Carefully cut art images from out-of-date art resource catalogs.

▶ Distribute the art images to students.

▶ For younger students, prepare mat board or poster board mounts for the images. Cut the mounts slightly larger than the images. Older students should cut their own mounts.

▶ Create or reproduce an art response journal and distribute to students.

▶ Encourage students to consult art books, websites, magazines, encyclopedias, and other resource materials for pertinent information about the art and artist. Allow about a week for the entire process.

▶ Provide class time for students to share their opinions about the artwork and what they have learned about the art and artist.

Any number of meaningful connections and extensions between visual arts and other subject areas can be made. For example:

▶ In the math classroom, students can graph information such as how many works of art fit a certain style, how many represent a particular culture, or how many fall into a specific time period. Reproduce the graph found in the Art and Mathematics chapter of *Bridging the Curriculum through Art* or create your own for this activity.

▶ In social studies, the art pins can be placed on world maps to indicate the area of the world where the original art object was made. Students can also place the art pins on a timeline to indicate the time period the original art object was made. Use the Venn Diagram found in the Art and Language Arts chapter to contrast and compare artwork and media from around the world and through time.

▶ In the language arts classroom, descriptive paragraphs can be written that elaborate upon the content of the artwork, the media or tools used, or other relevant art topics.

▶ In the performing arts studios, ask students to determine which art pins represent dance, drama, or music. Why would an artist choose to represent another art form? How is the performing art form represented in the art image?

Resources

Dobbs, S.M. *Learning in and Through Art: A Guide to Discipline-Based Art Education*.

Wilson, B. *The Quiet Evolution: Changing the Face of Arts Education*. The Getty Education Institute for the Arts, Los Angeles, 1997.

Art Journal

1. Write two or more sentences that tell your own opinion about the artwork on your art pin.

2. Wear your art pin everywhere you go. Record three or more questions or statements other people make about the artwork or artist.

3. Record three or more questions or statements that you have about the artwork or artist.

4. Look at the questions and statements other people made about the artwork or artist. What question or statement was made the most? Why do you think this was a frequent question or statement?

5. What is the title of the artwork?

6. When was it made?

7. Who made the artwork?

8. Where was it created?

9. When did the artist live?

10. What other information have you learned about the artwork and artist?

11. Write two or more sentences that tell your own opinion about the artwork on your art pin. How has your opinion changed?

Art Department Brochure

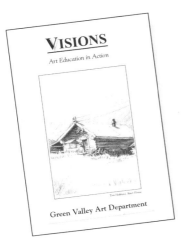

VISIONS
Art Education in Action

Green Valley Art Department

Art Department Brochure

Consider that the art program is much like any other special service that needs to be advertised to the public. One way to publicize the program is to create a brochure. Similar to commercial brochures, brochures about an art program should point out those items of significant interest to other teachers, administrators, parents, and community partners.

These are some suggested topics for art program brochures:

▶ Describe the goals and objectives of the program and highlight how those goals and objectives have been met, are being met, or are anticipated to be met.

▶ Identify the key players such as art teachers and administrators and the roles that each play.

▶ Promote the art teacher. Write a paragraph that highlights professional accomplishments including degrees held, membership in organizations, professional presentations, honors, and awards.

▶ Point out significant events scheduled throughout the year such as art exhibitions, performances, or special events for parents and the community.

▶ Identify community partners that support the art program through contributions of time or gifts.

▶ Recognize any outstanding art students such as those who have won competitions or have work in exhibitions.

To create the brochure, use any variety of desktop publishing software. Three-fold brochures are easy to make with computer software. Keep in mind that the art department brochure is the art department's professional face. Consider these pointers when designing and publishing the brochure:

▶ Use one style of easy-to-read font for unity and clarity.

▶ For variety and interest, use two sizes of the same font and add an occasional quote.

▶ Keep the information brief and concise. Too much text is not inviting to readers.

▶ Print the brochure on an eye-catching paper.

▶ Include an art image on the cover, preferably a student-produced artwork.

Distribution of the brochures should be as expansive as possible.

▶ Attend teacher meetings, school board meetings, or other public forums and provide brochures to everyone there.

▶ Send copies to the local newspaper and community organizations.

▶ Provide a basket of brochures for the school's office so that brochures are handy for new students and parents or visitors to the building.

▶ Furnish brochures for school administrative offices that are off campus.

▶ Create an online brochure to post to the school or district's website

Art Department Newsletter

Art Pins and Art Response Journal

Art Department Brochure

Art Department Newsletter

Exhibitions

Family Art Educational Evening

Art Department Newsletter

Similar to the art department brochure, a newsletter becomes a public face for the art program. Unlike the brochure, however, the newsletter is ongoing and can report timely events while keeping the readership — teachers, administrators, parents, and the community — updated on happenings within the art department.

Before beginning a newsletter, there are several points to consider. Determine:

▶ What software is available and can be used to create the newsletter?

▶ How often will the newsletter be published?

▶ How many pages will be produced each time?

▶ Who will assist with the gathering of information, writing of articles, copying, and distribution of the newsletter?

▶ How will funds be generated or acquired to publish the newsletter?

▶ Who will be the audience?

▶ Should text be published in more than one language?

Many desktop publishing software packages are available that contain newsletter templates. Although the first few issues of an elementary newsletter can be teacher-generated, later in the school year older students can assist with gathering information and writing articles. Secondary newsletters can become the responsibility of art club members or other groups.

When determining how often the newsletter is to be published, decide the timeline in advance and maintain a publication calendar. Your audience will learn to anticipate art department news if the newsletter is published on a regular schedule. When setting the publication calendar, try to find times when there are not many additional events happening. Avoid holidays and grade reporting periods as a time to publish the newsletter.

Try to maintain the same approximate number of pages with each issue. Also maintain the same heading, format, and font. The length of the newsletter will establish the cost of its production. Approach building administrators, parent-teacher organizations, or community business partners to underwrite the cost of one or more issues of the newsletter.

Determining the audience is as simple as asking who should know about the art program. Include teachers, parents, administrators, community organizations, and other community partners on the distribution list. Keep extra copies in the school office for visitors to read. Post the newsletter to the school or district website.

Exhibitions

Exhibitions

When it comes to showcasing the achievements of students in art, nothing is perhaps more traditional than art displays. What art teacher hasn't taped or stapled or tacked student work to hallway walls or bulletin boards? Taking those typical displays to a more professional level, however, better promotes the worth of the students' work while also placing the art department itself in a significantly more professional light.

▸ Consider hallways and bulletin boards as something more than just a place to display student work. Consider these exhibition spaces to be the walls of a gallery or museum. As such, student work should be treated with respect. Use great care in both preparation for exhibition and in display of the artwork.

▸ An investment in mats — whether inexpensively cut from construction paper or more expensively cut from mat board — provides a professional finished look for exhibitions.

▸ When displaying matted works on walls, space them at least an inch or more apart. Avoid using staples or tacks that go through the work itself. Try using pushpins as an alternative to staples or tacks.

▸ Write wall text that briefly explains the assignment and connections to other content areas. Display this wall text in a prominent area near the student exhibition.

▸ If reproductions of masterworks were used with the assignment, display those near the student work. Write a brief explanation about how the masterwork was explored during the lesson.

▸ Display students' written work with their artworks.

▸ Change student exhibitions often. Leaving the same work displayed for weeks on end loses much of the impact.

▸ Take student artwork on a traveling exhibition to the community. School district administration offices, public libraries, and city offices often have space for student exhibitions. Professional preparation of student work is doubly important in these arenas, as many more people will view the artwork.

Family Art Education Evening

Art Pins and Art Response Journal

Art Department Brochure

Art Department Newsletter

Exhibitions

Family Art Education Evening

Photo by Nancy Walkup.

Family Art Education Evening

An evening of art education activities provides parents, administrators, and other community members with opportunities to see firsthand what a comprehensive art program is all about. Involving the entire faculty and parent/student teams, an art education evening demonstrates integrated learning in a hands-on way.

To plan an art education evening, ground rules must be set. These rules should include:

▶ Students can only attend with a parent, guardian, or other adult.

▶ Students will act as guides or hosts through the interdisciplinary art activities.

▶ Parent/student teams will follow a rotating schedule.

▶ The evening is *not* designed for parent conferences.

▶ An art education evening is best implemented on a school night.

▶ About 90 minutes is required for successful implementation of an art education evening, with each activity taught for about 15 to 20 minutes.

▶ Ask grade-level or subject-area teams of teachers to host and teach one art-based activity such as those activities found in *Bridging the Curriculum through Art*.

▶ Provide any necessary materials, art resources, and instructions to the teacher teams. Provide a sufficient number of copies of written instructions and handouts for teachers to distribute to parent-student teams.

▶ Designate a registration area where a sign-in sheet can be maintained. If possible, provide a folder for parent-student teams to keep their handouts as they pass through each activity.

▶ Each activity should be taught in accordance with the rotating schedule with parent/student teams experiencing each activity for about 15 to 20 minutes before moving to the next station. Not all stations need to be visited by every parent-student team.

▶ Arrange the art room or other area to be the school art museum. Display student work throughout the room. Select older students to act as docents who will lead parent/student teams through the exhibition while providing information about each art object.

▶ Send invitations to parents, guardians, and other community members. Invite district administrators. Call the newspaper for coverage of the event.

Vocabulary

Activity   That part of the lesson that produces an end product such as a critical review, aesthetic discussion, historical timeline, or work of art. In art, an activity should reflect one of the four foundational disciplines of art while meeting stated objectives and aligning with local, state, or national content standards.

Alignment   Orderly and continuous matching of parts of a unit of study such as alignment of content to national and state standards or alignment of objectives with assessment strategies

Art-Based   Reference to activities, lessons, or units of studies that maintain meaningful exploration of art objects as central to the learning objective; also called "art-centered"

Aesthetics   A foundational discipline of art that deals with the philosophy of art or the "big" questions such as "What is art?"

Art Criticism   A foundational discipline of art that deals with description, analysis, judgment-making, and interpretation in relation to finding meaning in art objects

Art History   A foundational discipline of art that deals with time, culture, and place

Assessment   A measurement of learning achievement. Assessment should always align with objectives; therefore, objectives should be measurable.

CAE   Acronym for Comprehensive Art Education; the same concept as Discipline-Based Art Education

Checklist   A list that includes specific and usually sequential steps of a lesson or activity and sometimes has a rating scale for points awarded for each step. Checklists are often confused with rubrics, but they are not the same things. A checklist for creating a drawing might look something like this:

Used 10 or more details	20 points
Included a horizon line	10 points
Used color to show depth	25 points
Neat, complete, and on time	45 points
Total score	_____

Correlation   Material that is similar from content area to content area (e.g., music and art vocabulary are often the same; musicians and artists are generally classified using the same style labels such as pop, impressionist, or neo-classical)

Vocabulary

DBAE   Acronym for Discipline-Based Art Education, an approach to teaching that utilizes finding meaning in works of art through exploration of the four foundational disciplines of art: aesthetics, art criticism, art history, and art production

Goal   A broad-based end product (for example, students will learn about a well-known artist)

Integration   Material that is substantiated or threaded from one content area to another (e.g., the time, place, and culture of an artist is often recorded in the artist's work)

Lesson   An individual section of a unit of study that contributes to deeper exploration of a theme. Lessons are not necessarily time-sensitive and can cover more than one class session. An art-based lesson should include investigation of an artist and work of art, measurable objectives aligned with appropriate assessment, alignment with state and national content standards for art, and integration with one or more other content areas

Meaningful exploration   The key concept of CAE or DBAE is finding meaning in works of art. Finding meaning in all content areas provides opportunities for deeper exploration of concepts

National Content Standards   What students should know and be able to do in every content area of the curriculum and in every grade level; the National Content Standards were developed for each subject area by experts in each respective field of study and should be considered guidelines for development of challenging curricula

Objective   A measurable performance (for example, students will actively respond to philosophical questioning with well-supported reasons in regard to the strengths and weaknesses of an artist's work); objectives should always align (match) with assessment and the lesson's activity

Production   A foundational discipline of art that deals with the making of art objects

Rubric   Rubrics are sometimes confused with checklists; however, rubrics are much broader in scope. Whereas a checklist includes information about the ordered steps required for completing an activity, a rubric provides a range of learning expectations (for example; novice, competent, or exceptional) and further defines the criteria for each expectation.

Here is a sample of a rubric designed for a unit of study that includes four lessons.

Objective	Novice	Competent	Exceptional
Students will:			
consider an artist's personal history in relation to world events	Does not consider and cannot offer factual support for connecting the artist's personal history to world events	Identifies and offers limited factual support for connecting the artist's personal history to world events	Identifies and offers a variety of support for connecting the artist's personal history to other world events
identify ideas, analyze content and artistic intent, and communicate persuasive interpretations about the artist's work	Does not identify ideas, analyze content and artistic intent, and communicate persuasive interpretations about the artist's work	Uses limited support to identify ideas, analyze content and artistic intent, and communicate persuasive interpretations about the artist's work	Offers a variety of support to identify ideas, analyze content and artistic intent, and communicate persuasive interpretations about the artist's work
respond to philosophical questioning with compelling reasons in regard to the value, strengths, or weaknesses of the artist's work	Responds to philosophical questioning without reasons in regard to the value, strengths, or weaknesses of the artist's work	Responds to philosophical questioning with limited reasons in regard to the value, strengths, or weaknesses of the artist's work	Responds to philosophical questioning with well-supported reasons in regard to the value, strengths, or weaknesses of the artist's work
demonstrate an understanding of the connection between the artist's work and global events	Does not demonstrate an understanding of the connection between the artist's work and global events	Demonstrates a limited understanding of the connection between the artist's work and global events	Demonstrates a clear understanding of the connection between the artist's work and global events

Vocabulary

Theme Themes, as opposed to topics, are broad concepts or connecting ideas that typically are stated as a phrase or sentence and include an action verb

Topic A topic, as opposed to a theme, is narrow in scope (for example, pumpkins, seasons, or elephants) and will not lend itself to deep or meaningful exploration across the curriculum

Unit of study A series of lessons; art-based or art-centered units of study use the meaningful exploration of art objects as the bridge that connects all content areas

References

Books and Articles

Barrett, T. *Talking about Student Art*. Davis Publications: Worchester, MA, 1997.

Baum, A. and Baum, J. (1989). *Opt: An Illusionary Tale*. Viking Press.

Beyer, J. (1999). *Designing Tessellations: The Secrets of Interlocking Patterns*. Contemporary Books.

Birren, Faber. (1987). *Principles of Color: A Review of Past Traditions and Modern Theories of Color Harmony*. Schiffer Publishing.

Brown, K. (1998). *Poems about Science and Mathematics*. Milkweed Editions.

Buzan. Tony, and Buzan, Barry. (1996). *The Mind Map Book: How to Use Radiant Thinking to Maximize Your Brain's Untapped Potential*. Plume.

Consortium of National Arts Education Associations. (1994). *National Standards for Arts Education: What Every Young American Should Know and Be Able to do in the Arts*. Reston, VA: Music Educators National Conference.

Corn, M. Lynne. (1993). *Ecosytems, Biomes, and Watersheds: Definitions and Use*. Committee for the National Institute for the Environment.

Council for Basic Education. (1995, October 11). Review panels find history standards worth revising. News release submitted for publication.

Crafton, Linda K. (1996). *Standards in Practice: Grades K-2*. Urbana, IL: National Council of Teachers of English.

Dixon, N., Davies, and Politano, C. *Building Connections: Learning with Readers Theatre*. Peguis Publishers Ltd., Winnipeg, Canada, 1996.

Dobbs, S.M. *Learning in and Through Art: A Guide to Discipline-Based Art Education*.

Dunlap, R.A. (1998). *The Golden Ratio and Fibonacci Numbers*. World Scientific.

Finkel, N. and Finkel, L. (1980). *Kaleidoscope Designs and How to Create Them*. Mineola, NY: Dover Publications.

Greenberg, J. and Jordan, S. (1998). *Chuck Close Up Close*. New York: DK Publishing, 1998

Grun, Bernard. (1991). *The Timetables of History: A Horizontal Linkage of People and Events*. Simon and Schuster.

Hargittai, I. and Hargittai, M. (1996). *Symmetry: A Unifying Concept*. Shelter Publications.

Hellemans, Alexander, and Bunch, Bryan. (1991). *The Timetables of Science: A Chronology of the Most Important People and Events in the History of Science*. Simon and Schuster.

Herz-Fischles, R. (1998). *Mathematical History of the Golden Number*. Dover Publications.

Hirsch, E. D., Jr. (1987). *Cultural Literacy: What Every American Needs to Know*. Boston: Houghton Mifflin Company.

History standards project opens door to revisions. (1995, January 17). *Education Daily, 28*, 1-2.

International Baccalaureate. (1992). *Language A1 Guide*. Geneva, Switzerland: Author.

Holden, A. (1991). *Shapes, Space, and Symmetry*. Dover.

Jennings, T. (1998). *101 Amazing Optical Illusions: Fantastic Visual Tricks*. Sterling Publications.

Kendall, J. S., & Marzano, R. J. (1996). *Content Knowledge: A Compendium of Standards and Benchmarks for K-12 Education*. Aurora, CO: Mid-continent Regional Education Laboratory.

Kennedy, J. and Thomas, D. (1989). *Kaleidoscope Math*. Creative Publications.

Linn, Robert L. (1995). *Assessment-Based Reform: Challenges to Educational Measurement*. (William H. Angoff Memorial Lecture Series). Princeton, NJ: Educational Testing Service.

References

McIntosh, S. (1997). *The Golden Mean Book & Caliper Set*. Now and Zen.

Mager, Robert F. (1962). *Preparing Instructional Objectives*. Palo Alto, CA: Fearon Publishers.

Merian, M.S. (1991). *Flowers, Butterflies, and Insects*. New York: Dover Publications, Inc.

Marzano, R.J., & Kendall, J.S. (1996). *A Comprehensive Guide to Designing Standards-based Schools, Districts, and Classrooms*. Aurora, CO: Mid-continent Regional Educational Laboratory

National Assessment of Educational Progress Arts Education Consensus Project. (1994). *Arts Education Assessment Framework*. Washington, DC: National Assessment Governing Board.

National Center for History in the Schools. (1994a). *National Standards for History for Grades K-4: Expanding Children's World in Time and Space*. (Expanded ed.). Los Angeles: Author.

National Center for History in the Schools. (1994b). *National Standards for United States History: Exploring the American Experience*. (Expanded ed.). Los Angeles: Author.

National Center for History in the Schools. (1994c). *National Standards for World History: Exploring Paths to the Present*. (Expanded ed.). Los Angeles: Author.

National Center for History in the Schools. (1996). *National Standards for History*. (Basic ed.). Los Angeles: Author

National Commission on Excellence in Education. (1983). *A Nation at Risk: The Imperative for Educational Reform*. Washington, DC: Government Printing Office.

National Council for the Social Studies. (1994). *Expectations of Excellence: Curriculum Standards for Social Studies*. Washington, DC: Author.

National Council of Teachers of English and the International Reading Association (October, 1995). *Standards for the English Language Arts*. (Draft). Urbana, IL: National Council of Teachers of English.

National Education Goals Panel. (1991). *The National Education Goals Report: Building a Nation of Learners*. Washington, DC: Author.

National Research Council. (1996). *National Science Education Standards*. Washington, DC: National Academy Press.

The Oxford Treasury of Time Poems. (1998). Oxford University Press.

Rosen, J. (1998). *Symmetry Discovered: Concepts and Applications in Nature and Science*. Dover.

Runion, G. E. (1990). *Golden Section*. Dale Seymour Publications.

Seymour, D. and Britton, J. (1989). *Introduction to Tessellations*. Palo Alto, California: Dale Seymour Publications.

Stephens, P.G. and Green, S.D. (1997, November). Deciphering fact & opinion. *SchoolArts*, 40 - 41.

Simon, S. (1984). *The Optical Illusion Book*. William Morrow.

Stevens, P. S. and Smith, C.P. (1992). *Handbook of Regular Patterns: An Introduction to Symmetry in Two Dimensions*. MIT Press.

Sturgis, A. (1996). *Optical Illusions in Art*. New York: Sterling Publishing Co., Inc.

Wilcox, Michael. (1994). *Blue and Yellow Don't Make Green*. North Light Books.

Wilson, B. *The Quiet Evolution: Changing the Face of Arts Education*. The Getty Education Institute for the Arts, Los Angeles, 1997.

Study Prints

Interdisciplinary Connections: Take 5 Art Print series, Crystal Productions, 800-255-8629.

Take 5 Art Prints, Crystal Productions, 800-255-8629.

References

Videos

Chuck Close: A Portrait in Progress. Home Vision Arts, 4411 N. Ravenswood Ave., Third Floor, Chicago, IL 60640-5803.

The Fantastic World of M.C. Escher. Atlas Video.

Tessellations: How to Create Them (with artist Jim McNeill). Crystal Productions. 800-533-2847

Websites

http://www.ARTeaches.com
   Professional development programs for art education

http://www.crystalproductions.com
   Art education resources available from Crystal Productions

http://ditto.com
   Search engine that seeks images rather than text

http://members.aol.com/JMcne76382/home.html
   Samples of computer-generated tessellations created by artist Jim McNeill

http://www.bio2.edu/
   Website of Biosphere 2 in Arizona

http://www.mcrel.org
   Comprehensive listing of the national content standards as well as benchmarks and links to other sites

http://www.nhm.ac.uk/info/links/bot.htm
   Links to many botany-related sites

http://www.nmwa.org/legacy/bios/bmerian.htm
   Botanical artist Maria Sibylla Merian at the National Museum of Women in the Arts

http://www.storyarts.org/
   Curriculum ideas exchange, articles, and links for using storytelling in the classroom

Acknowledgements

The authors wish to thank the following persons for their contributions to *Bridging the Curriculum through Art: Interdisciplinary Connections*.

Brownsville Independent School District, Texas
Art teachers (Art pin)

Fort Worth Independent School District, Texas
Elizabeth Harris Willett, Alice Carlson Applied Learning Center (Family art education evening)

Hurst-Euless-Bedford Independent School District, Texas

Susan Dilleshaw Green, Bedford Heights Elementary (Fact and opinion)

Plano Independent School District, Plano, Texas
Michelle Mattoon, Mitchell Elementary (Newsletter and brochure)

Texas Woman's University, Denton, Texas
Sharon Warwick (timeline of art materials)

University of Florida Gainesville, Florida
Craig Roland (art of camouflage)

University of North Texas, Denton, Texas
Heather Murray, Graduate Research Assistant